Praise

"In this bold and informative manifesto, Susan Osborn argues that incest is not merely a private family tragedy or a rare psychological aberration. It is a deeply embedded system of power—sustained by institutional complicity and the strategic discrediting of those who speak. Osborn exposes how Western social structures, particularly the medical establishment, rush to contain it. The result is a powerful machinery of disbelief that preserves hierarchy and suppresses knowledge. Clear-eyed and incisive, *She's Such a Liar* reframes incest as a problem of knowledge and power—and calls for a collective reckoning with the systems that make truth dangerous."

—Jennifer Joy Freyd, Ph.D., Professor Emerit, Psychology, University of Oregon; founder and president, Center for Institutional Courage

"*She's Such a Liar* is a seismic indictment of the powerful cultural, medical, and political systems that have kept incest hidden for centuries. Brave, incisive, and grounded in extensive research, Susan Osborn, Ph.D., names the truth most institutions refuse to confront, tearing the veil off a hidden epidemic and demanding we finally face what so many endure behind closed doors. Long overdue, this is an unflinching call to confront the entrenched systems that protect abusers and silence survivors."

—Regina M. Calcaterra, Esq., *New York Times* best-selling author of *Etched in Sand*

"A tour de force. Osborn's book exposes the medical suppression of incest and the institutional forces that have sustained it for centuries. Meticulously researched and elegantly argued, this book confronts the politics of trauma and shame, dismantles the myth of medical neutrality, and calls for a cultural reckoning. This book could not be more timely."

—Dawn Skorczewski, Professor of English emerita, Brandeis University, author of *An Accident of Hope: The Therapy Tapes of Anne Sexton*

"Reading *She's Such a Liar* will make you furious. And then it will make you an activist. Susan Osborn's manifesto peels back centuries of male supremacist rhetorical and juridical strategies that have ever so conveniently invisibilized the father's role in perpetrating incest. Persuasively arguing that incest is not the medical problem of wayward girls but a systemic form of gender oppression, Osborn gives us the tools to dismantle the dominant discourses that continue to protect perpetrators at the expense of girls' human dignity."

—Marcie Bianco, author of *Breaking Free: The Lie of Equality and the Feminist Fight for Freedom*

"Osborn shows us in a beautifully written, concise volume that sexual violence against women, including incest, will never be solved until we lift the veil on the systems that support it. She invites us to rebuild a new culture that supports the equality of all, and disavows such violence completely and once and for all."

—Susan Prout, cofounder, I Have the Right To

"Meticulously researched and thoughtfully written, *She's Such a Liar* provides a vital and illuminating examination of how incest has been silenced across literature, medicine, and culture. Essential reading for feminists, clinicians, researchers, and advocates working in trauma and abuse recovery."

—Heidi Yewman, author of *Dumb Girl*

"Susan Osborn is an unstoppable force. Her latest book, *She's Such a Liar*, is a bold analysis of the systems that use sexual violence to oppress and subordinate women. I hope this work will be adopted by women's studies and gender studies departments globally."

—Liz Alterman, author of the award-winning memoir *Sad Sacked*

"*She's Such a Liar* is the phrase too many survivors hear when they tell the truth. Susan Osborn confronts the silence around incest and the systems that have helped keep it hidden."

—Babs Walters, author *Facing the Jaguar: A Memoir of Courage and Confrontation*

SHE'S SUCH A LIAR

INCEST KNOWLEDGE & POWER

A MANIFESTO

SUSAN OSBORN, PH.D.

Shake the Table Press
2801 B Street #111
San Diego, CA 92102

Book Cover and Interior Design by Monkey C Media
Author photo by Robin Resch

First Edition
Printed in the United States of America

Paperback ISBN: 979-8-9997766-0-0
eBook ISBN: 979-8-9997766-1-7

Library of Congress Control Number: 2026904253

For Margaret

CONTENTS

"The offender is not out of the ordinary. He did not land from an alien planet. He came from amongst us … and is a mirror of our culture."
—Linda Tschirhart Sanford

"People in power don't easily give up power."
—Alicia Ostriker

PREFACE

WOMEN IN THE WEST have much to be thankful for, let's not forget. My mother was born the year that women's suffrage was passed, a right denied generations before her. She lived to see the first woman nominated by a major political party to run as its candidate for president. Although she didn't always share Secretary Hillary Clinton's policy ideas, she was proud to have played a role in some of the extraordinary changes of the 20th century. She regretted not earning a college degree, but she became a commanding advocate for educational reform and students' rights. She was the first woman elected to our town's board of education, and she successfully argued for a student representative to be appointed to the board. During the late '60s and '70s, she opened her house to those of us involved in publishing an alternative school newspaper so we could make known our views about women's rights, civil rights, and the Vietnam War, all topics censored by our Nixonian high school principal. I have no doubt that for many in our young group, she was *the* model political activist: strategic, forceful, and often uncompromising.

But she also recognized that full equality, especially between women and men, was a long way off, and that there were causes for frustration as well as celebration. She often became enraged when she read board meeting minutes and discovered that her words had been tweaked, overlooked, or, most disturbingly, attributed to a man. Although she would have been puzzled by the notion of "women's history" and might even have dismissed it as unnecessary, she was acutely aware that her censure concealed a well of thick, choking injustices. Yet she counseled patience.

But it is hard to be patient with our culture's long-standing silence about sexual violence against women and girls. This silence is seen in especially high relief when it comes to incest.

My mother was often in my thoughts when I started researching this book. I wanted to get behind the powerful emotions that are too often used to dismiss discussion of incest (and other forms of sexual violence against girls and women) and to figure out how I would explain to her and millions of other women—and to myself—how deeply embedded are the institutional mechanisms and cultural forces that keep us from seeing, and dealing with, the reality of incest.

What I found surprised me. When it comes to covering up incest, Western culture has had thousands of years of practice.

PART 1

The Medical Suppression of Incest (i)

 about incest?

I get that incest is a difficult topic to talk about. Some think it's too dangerous or too icky and disgusting to talk about. Researchers and social service agencies Clorox it until it's unrecognizable. Serious talk show hosts head for the hills when the subject comes up. Even feminists tend to leave it out of discussions about sexual violence. You can't even find much about incest in medical literature despite the last fifty years of research documenting its prevalence and injurious impact; remarkably, doctors haven't even made sexual abuse histories a routine part of their clinical intake and diagnostic formulations. And daughters are the last ones who want to speak up about incest, either because their gender training has smothered them or simply because they know they may pay a very high price for being heard.

The rare time we do hear about incest, it always takes place in The Land of Far Away. Austrian monsters like Josef Fritzl who lock their daughters in underground bunkers and exploit them for decades commit incest,

1. This statue leaves no doubt about what is about to happen to Dymphna, patron saint of incestuously abused women, after she refused her father's sexual demands. As in most representations of her last moments, her father's masculine savagery contrasts sharply with her feminine piety, serving as a heteronormative gender reminder.

as do Colombian sadists such as Arcedio Alvarez Quintero who sexually exploited his daughters *and* his daughters' daughters. And then of course there's always an occasional celebrity who's outed. All this distancing gives the impression that incest is a very high-end or low-end affair, something that happens in filthy outbuildings in faraway places or in the debauched terrain of the ultra-wealthy in high-stakes industries, both places very few of us will ever go. This lack of attention suggests incest is a marginal phenomenon, not worthy of sustained analysis or even of much consideration, certainly not a phenomenon central to human affairs. You might even think we had evolved beyond incest.

But in fact, incest is very common in the US. We know that American women experience rape or attempted rape in alarming numbers—approximately one in six. But few of us are aware that conservative data indicate that *at least* as many American daughters experience incest before they're eighteen. And that's only the tip of the iceberg: studies indicate that most cases of incest are never reported. Recent data from the Bureau of Justice Statistics indicate that for girls under twelve, nearly 50 percent of perpetrators were family members, most of whom were male.

Given these numbers, one wonders why we don't hear more about incest.

What interests me is the relationship between incest's powerful emotional and moral appeal and the

2. The young Dr. Freud, just as he was beginning to get his toes wet in the big boys' world of professional medicine and institutional politics.

cultural silence surrounding it. It's well known that plenty of guys surf the net for incest porn, but most of us—including the guys watching the porn and the advice columnists at men's magazines who counsel the guys watching the porn—agree that incest is morally abhorrent and criminally culpable.

My aim here is to take a wide view, a very wide view, of the culturally awkward relationship between the prevalence of incest in our society and some of the social factors that blind us to this. I'm hoping that a wide view will help us move beyond the simple charge of misogyny that we tend to fall back on rather glibly. Certainly, misogyny is one way of describing what's going on (and it would be really very hard to make a convincing case that incest does not have to do with male contempt for and hostility toward women). But if we want to better understand—and do something about—the fact that daughters are incestuously abused by their fathers (or father surrogates) in remarkably high numbers, we need to question the larger infrastructure and core systems, the ordinary material and institutional arrangements that support and maintain incest's invisibility.

To do so, I want to begin with the medical profession and the first major example of a physician telling a woman that she got it all wrong when she described being incestuously attacked. I'm referring to Sigmund Freud, of course, who began his career primarily listening to middle-class and upper-class white women talk

3. Freud was not the only one writing "fairy tales" at the time. Sándor Ferenczi, a colleague of Freud's, published his work on incest in Europe despite Freud's, and the profession's, objections. However, publication in Britain was suppressed, with Freud's blessing, after the president of the International Psychoanalytical Association (and accused sexual predator) Ernest Jones advised that Ferenczi's "tissue of delusions ... can only discredit psychoanalysis."

about being sexually violated by their fathers. Part of Freud's concern was the sheer number of women who reported incestuous abuse. He also recognized that their descriptions revealed a pattern of long-lasting and severe psychic damage. Freud attributed a great deal of psychic significance to these experiences, and he planned on publishing his findings. But he got cold feet after his ideas were met with silence when he presented them at the Society for Psychiatry and Neurology, and the head of the Department of Psychiatry at the University of Vienna warned him against publishing what sounded very much like a "fairy tale."

There's something faintly pitiful about Freud's outsized concern for himself expressed in a letter he wrote to his dear friend Wilhelm Fliess following the conference mortification: "I am as isolated as you could wish me to be: the word has been given out to abandon me, and a void is forming around me." But his experience is a good demonstration that right at the beginning of the modern medical profession, physicians worried that taking incest seriously might challenge their growing monopoly of competence. More than that, as the emerging psychiatric profession had it, an integral part of being a physician was learning to take control of and dominate women's speech. Once Freud renounced his "erroneous" ideas, he was readmitted into the professional society that had threatened to give him the boot.

One of the remarkable aspects of Freud's revised theory is its sheer ingenuity:

> Since childhood masturbation is such a general occurrence and is at the same time so poorly remembered, it must have an equivalent in psychic life. And, in fact, it is found in the fantasy encountered in most female patients—namely, that the father seduced her in childhood. This is the later reworking which is designed to cover up the recollection of infantile sexual activity and represents an excuse and an extenuation thereof. The grain of truth contained in this fantasy lies in the fact that the father, by way of his innocent caresses in earliest childhood, has actually awakened the little girl's sexuality ... It is these same affectionate fathers that are the ones who then endeavor to break the child of the habit of masturbation, of which they themselves had by that time become the unwitting cause. And thus the motifs mingle in the most successful fashion to form this fantasy, which often dominates a woman's entire life (seduction fantasy): one part truth, one part gratification of love, and one part revenge.

The British psychoanalyst Rosemary Balsam has aptly noted Freud's penchant for baroque reasoning, and it is tempting to take this apart bit by syntactical bit, but for the sake of concision, let's just say that Freud wasted a lot of time trying to say that incest never happens.

Freud's ingenuity was just the first in a long line of remarkably innovative and largely successful attempts by medical professionals to not only deny the reality of incest but also to distance fathers from all evidence of it by emphasizing their innocence. During the late 19th century and the first half of the 20th, for example, stumped physicians spent many sleepless nights trying to figure out how to explain away the nationwide epidemics of gonorrhea vulvovaginitis in very young girls.

Part of the problem was its sheer scale; once medical technologies such as germ theory, microscopes, and the Gram stain were developed, gonorrhea could be unequivocally identified, and epidemics of gonorrhea in young girls *were* identified in every geographic region of the country: New York, San Francisco, Los Angeles, Chicago, St. Louis, Philadelphia, Baltimore, Washington DC, and Boston. By 1927, gonorrhea in girls ranked as the second most common contagious disease in the country, second only to measles and outnumbering smallpox and scarlet fever. "Vulvovaginitis" in young girls was declared "the most neglected and poorly managed condition seen in [the history] of medical practice." In some city hospitals, girls were tucked three

4. He did it.

5. She did it.

to a bed; many more were turned away. Physicians were baffled. They had long known that gonorrhea was a venereal disease—Hippocrates formulated this fact in the 5th century BCE—but how it got into little girls was anyone's guess.

Part of the challenge—as it had been with Freud—was trying to make sense of the enormous number of middle-class and upper-class white girls living in posh parts of towns who were infected. The physicians' descriptions are revealing. "It is trying to our credulity," explained one stumped hospital superintendent, "to find a 4-year old daughter and a 35-year old father having gonorrhea at the same time with no other source of infection to the daughter other than the father, and yet I have observed this in a family of educated and refined people." Head-scratching physicians across the country echoed his incredulity: "[O]ne is occasionally utterly unable to trace the source of infection in a child surrounded by every protection and comfort money can procure."

In the face of infections they could neither explain nor ignore, medical experts proliferated a remarkable number of hypotheses to explain away the epidemics and punt responsibility away from the obvious. When the cast of usual scapegoats—Black men, dark-skinned immigrants, and poor men living in crowded tenements—fell flat, physicians, researchers, and public health policy experts reprised Freud's innocence idea and floated the "accidental," a.k.a. "innocent," transmission idea. It's not what you think, asserted the president of the Chicago Pediatric Society and the American Pediatric Society. Rather, it's a matter of "dangerous things," declared a renowned physician and public health policy expert: sponges, towels, thermometers, soap, and bathwater were the perpetrators. Another earnest physician at New York City's Metropolitan Hospital and Dispensary for Women and Children repeated the alarm and added bedclothes, cotton pads, and rags to the list of the malignly disposed. Other savants insisted that mothers were the offenders: "[T]he child victims of gonorrhea usually have been infected by their mothers," asserted the original "dangerous things" theorist, who explained that mothers transmitted the disease via ordinary household items such as inadequately cleaned toilets, towels, washcloths, sponges, bathtubs, and fingers. "All objects … which are damp … should be regarded with utmost suspicion." Those who held onto the old-fashioned idea of personal transmission stood in the way of progress.

As ridiculous as all this seems, nobody was joking. It didn't matter that none of this made any sense or that the professionals' ideas contradicted their own empirical evidence. Each time new theoretical speculation gained credibility, public health officials and medical professionals issued new warnings and invented new ways to stop the spread of gonorrhea: mothers were to burn or discard infected girls' clothes, their bed linens were to be washed separately after first being saturated

6. At Babies Hospital in New York City, Dr. Emmett Holt, one of the country's most respected physicians, erected a new building to house infected girls, fumigated the walls, and put the girls in diapers. He also proposed changing the name of the disease to dissociate it from its "venereal origins." But even this rhetorical sleight of hand did not reduce the incidence of infection.

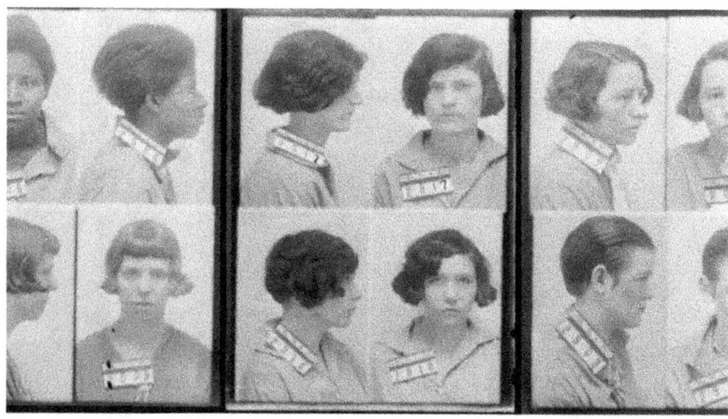

7. Teenage inmates incarcerated for gonorrhea and syphilis at the Kansas State Industrial Farm in 1926. As the epidemics continued unabated, overworked government officials did what they could to restrict "persons who were irresponsible and could not be trusted to safeguard others from infection." No effort was made to quarantine infected boys or men.

in a bichloride of mercury solution and boiled, and girls' hands were to be scrubbed with bath alcohol and their vaginas with boric acid followed by mercurochrome treatments. To further reduce susceptibility to infection, nurses recommended that mothers induce regular bowel movements and keep them from eating rich food. When those measures also failed to prevent the spread of gonorrhea, medical experts recommended that girls be quarantined, typically within their homes.

Over time, physicians and public health officials worried that the girls' infections threatened to subvert not just their own health, but the social and political stability—the health—of the whole state. The "detention, isolation, quarantin[ing], or commitment to institutions," wrote a board member of a distinguished public health agency, "may be found necessary for the protection of the military and naval forces of the United States against venereal diseases." To mitigate this ominous threat, local governments built special schools for infected girls. Others simply expelled them and banned them from skating rinks, swimming pools, and ball fields. Many hospitals built special isolation wards and marked the girls' beds with red warning ribbons. Across the country, city leaders elected to send infected girls to reformatories where they were treated as criminals along with the juvenile delinquents. To protect the forces preparing for war, prior to and during World War I, infected girls were often arrested and sent to one of forty-three prisons, politely known as "detention houses," where

8. The red ribbons tied to the infected girls' hospital beds invoked earlier eras when the color red was used to shame and mark women deemed sexually "sinful," such as Hester Prynne, the protagonist of Nathaniel Hawthorne's *The Scarlet Letter.*

they could "be studied." This, despite a surgeon general's report indicating that five-sixths of the men who went to enlist were infected prior to induction. By 1931, the idea of isolating the girls to protect the public and national health had won the imprimatur of the White House. However, none of these measures controlled the spread of gonorrhea any better than scrubbing daughters' vaginas, blaming mothers, or inducing regular bowel movements.

Despite the profession's ethic of neutrality and disinterestedness, the remarks of some physicians suggest that there was more at work here than just a misguided focus on sanitation. One particularly evocative comment by a leading physician at New York's Babies Hospital suggests that a more deeply rooted problem—sexual prejudice—might have clouded the professionals' judgment: The girls were like "Satan," he wrote, "serpent[s] who came in the form of a child."

Over time, the effort to eradicate gonorrhea in young girls must have seemed like a game of whack-a-mole; no sooner had one bone-headed theory been floated when another epidemic emerged and a sillier theory was run out. Along the way, the gonococcus bacterium was endowed with incredible powers of locomotion and survival, at least when a prepubescent girl was in the vicinity. For instance, in a somewhat desperate Hail Mary, Frederick Taussig, an early-20th-century gynecologist at the Washington University Hospital in

9. Physicians' offhand remarks, along with the lavish cleansing rituals prescribed to purify the girls' vaginas, suggest that ancient prejudices associating women with temptation, impurity, sexual danger, and sin lay just below the surface of the professionals' diagnostic efforts and may have influenced their decisions for controlling and treating the girls.

St. Louis, came up with a theory that rivaled Freud's in its ingenuity. Taussig suspected that "innocent" or fomite transmission was virtually impossible. But because the epithelial linings of very young girls' vulvas are thinner than those of adult women, Taussig speculated that the malignant bacteria penetrated the girls as they sat on the loo. To prevent self-contamination, he advocated lowering public toilet bowls and replacing O-shaped seats with U-shaped seats so that when the littlest users backed onto the seats, they would not infect themselves. How did a girl too young to use a toilet contract gonorrhea? That ticklish problem left everyone clueless.

Taussig's speculation was enthusiastically endorsed by the American Pediatric Society, which recommended U-shaped seats be installed in girls' and women's public lavs across the country. Government agencies quickly sent emissaries into the field to hunt down implicated O seats. But most of the time, they couldn't even confirm the existence of the maligned toilet, let alone verify that a girl had become infected while using one. At one address, a beleaguered seat hunter found only an empty lot. Yet in her report, she reaffirmed the party line: "[A]ll medical literature includes the toilet seat as a possible medium of infection … direct [sexual] contact is responsible for a minimum incidence of infection."

Taussig's theory and those of others in the medical community were about as plausible as Donald Trump's idea that bleach taken internally kills COVID-19 and

10. Photographed at the height of his career, Taussig looks less like an innovator and more like the president of a rather smug and punctilious stamp club.

about as rational as Freud's notion that girls fantasize about being raped by their fathers and then lie about it (or his striking notion that to develop normally, girls must give up their innate desire for a penis and then displace that desire into a wish to have a male baby). Whatever made someone in the medical community finally conduct empirical research into the viability of the toilet theory is anyone's guess. But it happened in 1938 when members of the New York City–based Vaginitis Project laced a toilet seat with gonorrhea bacteria and waited around to see how long the germs remained virulent. The results were compelling: Physicians agreed that in open air, gonorrhea bacteria dry before they can infect anyone. Examinations of patient records from multiple hospitals and child-caring institutions supported their findings. In fact, at one hospital, all the children, including girls infected with gonorrhea and those who were not, used the same toilets still outfitted with O-shaped seats. None of the girls who were not infected before arriving at the hospital became infected while in the hospital. The project's report unequivocally rejected the idea that girls could catch gonorrhea from toilet seats, but it held on to damp towels and bed linens. Later that year, when the 11th edition of the most prestigious pediatric textbook of the 20th century, *Holt's Diseases of Infancy and Childhood,* was published, it asserted that gonorrhea in girls was not to be regarded as a venereal disease. Fancy had finally become fact.

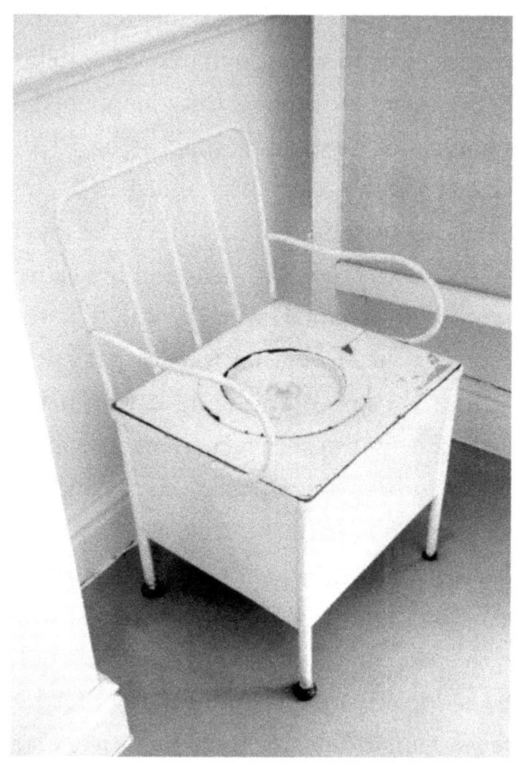

11. It did it.

PART 2

The Medical Suppression of Incest (ii)

 think we need to pause here and remember that this is a story about girls. It is not a story about boys. In fact, physicians of the time showed no hesitation identifying incest as the cause in the rare case of a boy's gonorrhea infection. But a father infecting his daughter through sexual contact? Well, that was another matter—and another etiology—altogether.

As disturbing as this story is, there's more here than first meets the eye. The profession's suppression of incest was not just a reflection of its resistance to acknowledging an uncomfortable fact. Nor can it be chalked up to prudery or the profession's awkward realization that sexual feelings don't always obey the mores of civilization. It was partly that. And it was also part of a desperate attempt to maintain the idea of virtue as an exclusive possession of white men, the newly minted "gentle-men" of the early 20th century, especially in the face of the threats presented by Reconstruction and the unprecedented advancement of Black people and immigrants of color. Before the 1890s, well-heeled white fathers—clergymen, physicians, governmental officials, farmers, and other wealthy elite—constituted the single largest group of men accused of incest. But after the Civil War, newspapers began proliferating reports about incest in families of color and destitute families. The lack of evidence supporting these claims was irrelevant to the professional white Americans eager to affirm their idea of the American dream. *The Washington Post*, for example, reported that incest was the "blackest and most savage of crimes" that Black men regularly commit. A powerful story was being told by white male power brokers about sexuality, race, and ethnicity in an attempt to cement white male privilege and power and to secure the idea of moral integrity as the exclusive, if not the defining, aspect of white men; the physicians' willingness to revise their ideas about infection but not incest reveals a deep engagement with and commitment to racist, sexist, and classist ideologies.

But we're also dealing with a much more loaded and insidious power grab on the part of the profession, and one with a much greater impact than we usually acknowledge on our own conventions and assumptions about incest and the silence that surrounds it. What I mean is that over time the medical officials' chain of contacts leading to the girls' infections led further and further away from the home and finally landed in all-female spaces, specifically girls' public lavatories where no fathers were permitted to go. In its own obtuse, audacious, and callous way, the medical profession's revision of the etiology of gonorrhea when the bacteria came in contact with prepubertal girls was about keeping common sense, women, science, or anything else from interfering with paternal authority in the home and the father's tacit and long-standing sexual rights to his daughters. Had the implications of the girls' infections been acknowledged, fathers' entitlement would be challenged and the truth would no longer be their property.

It's worth underscoring a point here. The persistence of the disease, the epidemic prevalence of particular symptoms in young girls across the country, and the failure of well-tested therapies to control their symptoms created a "crisis of cure" in the medical profession and forced physicians to the limits of their perception. The girls' symptoms were treated as legitimate medical problems at first, but when they did not respond to treatment, the girls became objects of medical and governmental control.

In the only book to date on the subject of the gonorrhea epidemics, Lynn Sacco's meticulously researched and scholarly *Unspeakable: Father-Daughter Incest in American History*, the author takes pains to suggest that the actions of the physicians, nurses, social workers, and public health officials weren't conspiratorial. In my more charitable moments, I want to agree with her. They weren't conspiratorial if we think about conspiracy in terms of conscious planning and secret agreements. But it is difficult to see how a rational person could lend credibility to the ideas concocted by the medical profession. While the spin may not have been the result of a conspiracy, the fact that the outlandish was embraced as truth suggests a certain complicity and, at the very least, a mutually supportive ideological collusion.

It would be reassuring to think the masculinist ideology that maintained the medical profession's dissembling was part of an anomalous and rather embarrassing moment in the history of medicine, a peculiar misogynistic blip on the human timeline. Distant in time it may be. But the effort to distance fathers from evidence of incest is part of an ongoing tradition of suppression by the still largely white medical and psychiatric professionals to which we are still subject. Let's not overstate the case. The suppression of incest cannot be wholly attributed to Freud or to the white male physicians working during the 19th and 20th centuries. There are all kinds of variant pressures and competing influences on us and our social and political systems, and the medical profession has thankfully overthrown many of the gendered certainties of the past. Yet it takes only a casual glance at contemporary medical and scientific journals to see that many of the themes I have been highlighting emerge again and again. Some recently published studies see in girls' gonorrhea infections another opportunity to indict mothers by reprising the "dirty things" theories. Another, published in the *New England Journal of Medicine,* details researchers' efforts to implicate public toilet seats, again. And in *The Pediatric Infectious Diseases Journal,* you can find a recent study reexamining the possibility of fomite or, as the researcher delicately writes, "bathroom spread" of gonorrhea in the case of two infected children under age five because their "home situations are not suggestive of sexual abuse." The now-discredited ideas of the False Memory Syndrome Foundation—a pseudo-scientific organization founded in 1992 by an elite mathematician, Peter Freyd, at the University of Pennsylvania to combat the "epidemic" of "false memories" of incest, including his own daughter's—are still successfully employed in courtrooms today. Perhaps most notoriously, Woody Allen's attorneys relied on them to challenge daughter Dylan Farrow's sexual abuse account and to malign her mother, Mia Farrow. More recently, in 2024, incest charges were dropped against a Purdue professor after his legal team argued that his daughters' charges of incest were made up, the result of "false memories" implanted in the daughters by a therapist.

And the list of dirty things? It just keeps getting longer and longer. In 2021, the *Journal of Medical Case Reports* published a study by a public health expert and a marine biologist implicating a thermal pool at the edge of Italy's crater lake Specchio di Venere as the probable source of an eleven-year-old girl's gonorrhea infection. Their study, based in part on discredited ideas from the 19th century and Taussig's notions about epithelial cells, also includes public health warnings and a photo of the lake with a link to enlarge the image of the pool in case you want to take a close-up look at the miscreant.

12. The lake did it.

The point here is simple but important: as far back as the beginning of modern medicine, we can see a radical separation between the reality of incest and the social construction of incest. One conspicuous example brings this right up to the present day.

Search the Centers for Disease Control and Prevention (CDC) pages for "Sexual Assault or Abuse of Children." Don't bother looking for their pages on incest; they don't have any. This august body that operates under the aegis of the Department of Health and Human Services admirably acknowledges a possible connection between evidence of sexually transmitted infections (STIs) in children and sexual violence. But the list of circumstances that might lead physicians to test for STIs reveals a glaring omission. Physicians are encouraged to consider testing if the child has experienced certain injuries, has been abused by a stranger or someone known to be infected with an STI, or lives in a community with a high rate of STIs. Only once does the CDC specifically refer to the possibility of incest: A physician is to consider testing if "[t]he child has a sibling, other relative, or another person in the household with an STI." Nowhere in its articles is the word "father" ever used, nor, if a quick Google search of the first ten pages of links to the CDC and child sexual assault is any indication, does the CDC use the word "incest" in all of its articles on sexual violence committed against children, except as required by references to sources outside itself. And never is the word "father" mentioned on these pages. What this absence underscores, of course, is a disconcerting ideological alliance between the medical profession and the state and a shared concern with preserving the dominant sexist values of society, including fathers' tacit sexual entitlement to their daughters.

My point here is that the blind spot that keeps us from seeing and talking about incest raises bigger questions and concerns than those that might emerge from an inspection of the private chambers of our minds, and those questions have to do with knowledge, power, and the collective interests of our culture's epistemological stakeholders. While we like to think of medicine as a neutral entity and trust that the profession's ethics of disinterestedness acquit it of capitalist profit motive and political biases—of the major professions, medicine has the greatest claim to an ideal of service and devotion to human welfare—what we see happening here is that its cognitive and normative elements have been and continue to be used ideologically. Institutional concerns about preserving patriarchal authority—inside and outside of the house—have had a much greater impact than we've previously acknowledged on why incest remains out of sight and unacknowledged. Going forward, if we want any hope of changing the situation, we need to examine not just individual doctors' acts of sexism, but how the medical profession has acted and continues to act as an extended patriarchy. And we need to engage in

- The child has experienced penetration or has evidence of recent or healed penetrative injury to the genitals, anus, or oropharynx.
- The child has been abused by a stranger.
- The child has been abused by an assailant known to be infected with an STI or at high risk for STIs (e.g., injecting drug user, MSM, person with multiple sex partners, or person with a history of STIs).
- The child has a sibling, other relative, or another person in the household with an STI.
- The child lives in an area with a high rate of STIs in the community.
- The child has signs or symptoms of STIs (e.g., vaginal discharge or pain, genital itching or odor, urinary symptoms, or genital lesions or ulcers).
- The child or parent requests STI testing.
- The child is unable to verbalize details of the assault.

13. Someone's gone missing.

much more analysis, both historical and contemporary, of how male dominance—its institutional and private forms of power and authority—works, changes, and endlessly reconfigures itself in different contexts and at different historical moments. We also need to think much harder about how resilient and powerful private, institutional, and political forces have helped engender the disempowering emotions—*including the daughter's shame, which is too often conceived as devoid of history, politics, and power*—that keep us from examining why incest remains the most common form of sexual violence in the country (and I suspect much of the rest of the world), and why prepubescent gonococcal vaginitis remains the most common form of gonorrhea in childhood.

So far in reflecting on the ordinary institutional concerns that keep us from seeing incest, I have followed the usual "bottom-up" path in discussions of this kind by moving from past historical facts and events to those of our own day. But I don't think that this model, while important and necessary, adequately speaks to the problem of incest, as it still treats the problem of incest too narrowly, largely correlating it with specific moments in our dark past that we hope (expect?) will be exceeded by more enlightened thinking in the future. While this beguiling notion of linear progress might hold true in certain areas such as engineering and technology—we could say that the invention of the gas motor engine led to the invention of the automobile; the invention of the microphone led to the invention of the telephone—the invention of penicillin in 1945 and its subsequent distribution did not cure incest or reduce its prevalence. To more deeply understand why incest is so hard to eradicate, then, we need to look beyond our conventional ideas about history and progress and think more about incest's cultural value as well.

While incest is committed against all genders, it is overwhelmingly a heterosexist crime; it is a crime committed against a girl *because* of her gender. From a very early age—the youngest girl admitted to a gonorrhea ward during the epidemics was three months old—incest trains a girl to be complicit with her own subordination. It brings to life all the miserable qualities associated with femininity including obedience, silence, passivity, loyalty, fear, docility, and deference. Philosophically speaking, incest gives a girl an existential stake in the injustices that subjugate her. It is her induction into the heterosexist sexual order; it initiates her life as a sexual subject, as a being that exists for men.

Put differently, incest is that process through which girls "internalize," that is, make as their own, a masculinist image of their sexuality *as* their identity as women. A girl who experiences incest "becomes a woman" not so much through a process of physical maturation, but rather through an experience of eroticized dominance that intertwines her physical, emotional, and social status in shame and degradation.

What I'm pointing to here is that incest is the primal scene where patriarchal culture's work is done. It's the way gender is inscribed on a girl's body. For tens of millions of girls, it is the way male dominance and female subordination are first established and enforced. Hardly a private, sordid family drama, incest is a practice that produces, reproduces, and naturalizes one of culture's founding presuppositions, that of gendered subjectivity and heterosexuality. What is at stake here, then, when we consider the prevalence of incest and its suppression, is the maintenance of the whole structure of unequal social relations, asymmetric power dynamics, and prejudicial ideologies that support and sustain patriarchal culture—the entire nexus of presuppositions about gender normativity and gender differences that structures heteropatriarchal culture. Far from standing on the periphery of culture, incest props it up from within.

Given the multifarious cultural pressures and influences that contribute to patriarchal society's subordination of women, this may seem excessively stated. But the long and continued suppression of incest strongly suggests that incest has been and continues to be a far more powerful influence on the social construction of heterosexuality than previously thought.

And that makes incest worth everyone's attention.

PART 3

Incest and the Politics of PTSD

I'D LIKE TO TURN now to the psychiatric profession and think more about the ways this subsection of the medical establishment has contributed to suppressing incest and politically disempowering women who have experienced incest and other forms of sexual violence. To do so, I want to start near the beginning of the modern psychiatric profession, with one of the first known examples of a doctor telling an incestuously abused girl that her account of the violent sexual assault she experienced was a manifestation of a bodily dysfunction, a disorder within her. It happened in Paris in October 1875 when a young mother dropped her fourteen-year-old daughter, Augustine, at the Salpêtrière Hospital and Asylum after she started displaying disturbing behaviors and an intractable and very unladylike anger.

Augustine wasn't amused by her confinement, and in front of the asylum's director, Jean-Martin Charcot, and his interns, she started yelling about fire, blood, her hatred of men, revolution, escape, and rape: "Get rid of the snake you have in your pants … It's a sin!" At which point, Charcot intervened. "You see how

14. While the purpose of this photo of the hospitalized Augustine is not clear, it may have been designed by Charcot to appeal to her emotions, a visual goad showing her what she could become if she abandoned her anger and returned to her "naturally" buttoned-up state of femininity.

hysterics scream," he blandly informed his interns as he chloroformed Augustine into unconsciousness. "Noise," he elaborated, "much ado about nothing."

There is something almost comic about this boorish old man showing off to his students in this draconian way. But it's a nice demonstration that right from the start of the modern medical profession, the voices of girls were not being heard. More than that, as Charcot had it, an integral part of a physician's job was to take control of the disorder within and subjugate the patient back into her "natural" state of feminine docility and obedience. To do so, he diagnosed Augustine with hysteria, a disease thought to be of the uterus. He treated the locus of Augustine's problem, her "hysterogenital" area, with compression, genital manipulation, and electrical shocks. As Charcot's treatments started to make Augustine's behavior less refractory, he added new treatment goals to assess and "fix" her "insanity." The first was to model highly eroticized poses, without complaint, so that he could use his camera to "objectively" record the "hysterical type." These photos were later published in his acclaimed medical text, *Iconographie photographique de la Salpêtrière.* Another of Charcot's sanity tests required naked patients to line up and parade before him so that he could get a more penetrating look at their hysterias. Augustine was also required to perform hysteria in front of crowds of intellectuals, dignitaries, and actors who filled the asylum's amphitheater during Charcot's weekly shows: Once hypnotized and scripted, she ate paper, barked like a dog, and waltzed with invisible men. When Augustine regressed and deviated from what was considered her naturally subservient state—she broke windows and repeatedly tried telling the dismissive physicians about her nightmares—she was once more shut up with chloroform or ether, straitjacketed, and locked in an isolated cell.

Today, it's hard to take such medical hijinks seriously. Hopefully, no medical professionals are working in psychiatric settings while summoning up their inner Jeffrey Epsteins and lining up naked female inmates to be ogled by groups of fellow physicians, members of the royal family, celebrity presidential candidates, and other distinguished spectators. The idea of today's medical men proving the "truth" of their science with the help of photos of stripped-down or dolled-up women is more than a little absurd. And it's hard to imagine any practicing physician humiliating a woman into complicity with a treatment plan by forcing her to participate in a degrading series of med school frat party stunts. Instead, 21st-century psychiatrists and medical doctors would most likely diagnose Augustine with post-traumatic stress disorder (PTSD) and recommend one-on-one talk therapy with a trained professional in the hope that during the process of discovering and talking through disturbing and unwanted feelings and thoughts, she would experience psychic and physical relief.

15. It was often said that if women weren't insane before entering the Salpêtrière, they certainly were when they came out. In the local press, Charcot was known as the "Napoleon of Neuroses," the "Caesar of the Salpêtrière"; he is still recognized as the father of modern neurology.

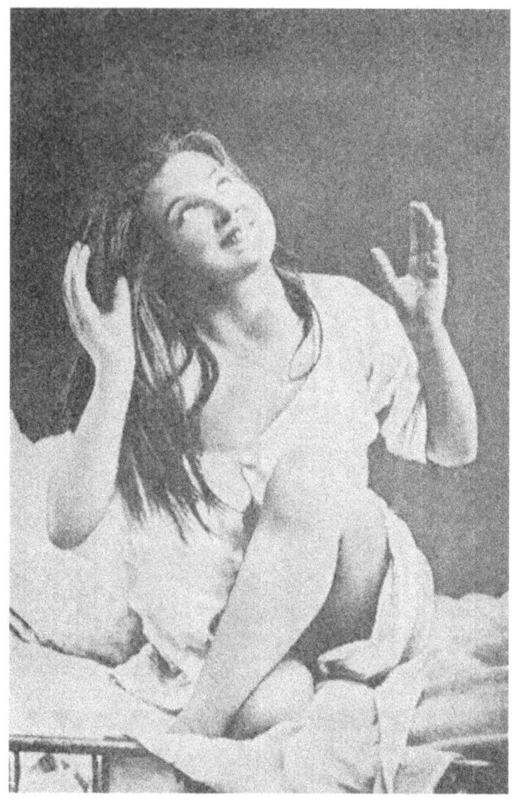

16. In this staged image of Augustine, the collusion of sexually loaded imagery, including the disheveled, bedhead hair and off-the-shoulder hospital gown, and the putative objectivity of photography, lends a sense of medical truth to Charcot's choreographed images.

17. Charcot's well-lit and carefully composed images seemed so indelibly real, so close to life, that for decades they were used to support clinical diagnoses. His use of photography "was as crucial to the study of hysteria as the microscope was to histology," gushed one infatuated observer of the time. Yet after visiting a similar asylum to get ideas for her roles, famed actor Ellen Terry complained that the madwomen she saw were much "too theatrical" to teach her anything.

18. When reflecting on Charcot's treatment plans, it's hard not to call up images of more recent patriarchal training grounds such as 1950s charm schools where young women were initiated into their new lives as sexual subjects by learning the arts of obedience and submission.

But before we congratulate ourselves on how far we've come, we need to think more about Charcot's treatment of Augustine and the bigger questions it points to about women's mental distress, the medical profession's treatments today, and incest. What are the historical underpinnings of misogyny in the profession? What kinds of misogyny and what words and images informed Charcot's treatment of Augustine? What stories has the profession told itself regarding women, in the West at least, for thousands of years, and how do those stories influence current thinking about women's psychic distress and treatment plans? What cultural myths about women are so deeply embedded in our minds and the profession that we don't even question them? And how might today's treatments ironically be contributing to the suppression and invisibilization of the very behavior they supposedly call attention to—incest?

Charcot's decision to interpret Augustine's troubles as "symptoms," signs of an illness, a manifestation of a malfunction within—*as she repeatedly emphasized*—as opposed to a response to an external event, was just one in a long line of largely successful attempts stretching back to ancient times not only to interpret women's psychic discontent and suffering as signs of a disease, but also to prove that the distress was caused by women's inherently unstable and undisciplined bodies and minds. Go back to ancient Greek myths, for example, and we find the Argonaut physician Melampus blaming "uterine melancholy" for the virgins' inexplicable desire to flee men's sexual and political demands. In the 4th century BCE, Aristotle, no slouch when it came to thinking about women's "deficiencies," taught that women's minds and bodies were second-rate ("mutilated" males) and ill-equipped for almost every human activity—you know which one he *did* reserve for women—by comparing their bodies with the naturally right stuff of men's. A century later, Hippocrates repeatedly returned to the idea of the unstable and obstreperous uterus as the cause of women's psychic and physical suffering. In his famous *Diseases of Women*, that extraordinary book of aphorisms and observations about infection and epidemiology (and one of the most influential medical works in the West), he explains that once the uterus becomes unhinged from its natural position, this headstrong and perversely independent organ takes a kind of pig-headed pleasure in violating its own order of health: it propels itself throughout a woman's body causing all sorts of chaos, including her propensity for irrational thinking and troublesome and difficult behavior. Aretaeus, the 2nd-century CE Roman physician, summed up the whole bothersome situation this way: "[The uterus] is like an animal within an animal."

Blatant, and tedious, misogyny? Of course. But the problem runs deeper than it first appears. Male culture's determination to mark women's bodies as deviant and their unhappiness and suffering as a sign of an illness, a malfunction of the individual, was not just about establishing the male body as the right,

19. Right from where written evidence of Western culture starts, medical men were doing everything they could to make sure that everyone knew who was rational and who wasn't. In this illustration from *Justi Cortnummii, De morbo attonito liber unus ad Hippocraticam*, a medical text published in 1677, we see the pioneering physician on the right and Galen, a second-century follower, on the left.

20. Throughout Western history, we find repeated emphasis on women's inherent bodily disorder in contrast to the orderly, rational male body, not just in medicine but in art and literature as well. In this late-19th-century painting, we see the representatives of sanity and reason, the men, all on one side of the painting and the representatives of insanity, the women, all on the other, their disordered minds and bodies, like Augustine's, quite literally exposed to—and opposed to—the authoritative eye of scientific male rationality.

21. By the mid-19th century, Shakespeare's Ophelia had become the medical profession's poster girl for the distressed, "hysterical" woman; as one medical savant wrote, "… Ophelia … is a copy from nature." Note the familiar use of certain visual symbols including the bedhead hair and the off-the-shoulder gown to represent the disordered female mind (see illustrations 16 and 17).

stable, and normative one. That was part of it. But we're dealing with a much more loaded and insidious power grab on the part of medical men, and one with a much greater impact than we usually acknowledge on our contemporary traditions, conventions, and assumptions about gender and health. What I mean is that the uterus was not just a body part that men didn't share. It was *the* part of human anatomy that defined femininity as a gender, the one that marked women's bodies as structurally hysterical. A woman not prey to insanity was, by definition, quite simply, not a woman. Or, as the ancient Romans used to say, "*Tota mulier in utero*": Woman is nothing but a uterus.

Of course, we don't talk in those bald terms now. Or not quite. For many aspects of this traditional package of views about women's inherent, biological defectiveness and propensity to mental disorder—a package going back in its essentials over multiple millennia—still underlie many medical professionals' assumptions about women's psychic suffering and discontent today. Take the language used by mainstream psychiatric professionals and traumatologists to describe women's psychic unrest, which is not that far off from Hippocrates's words or those of any of the other dogmatic and insolent physicians of the past. In making their case for diagnosing incestuously abused women with PTSD, what are those women said to be? "Disordered," only this time it's not women's uteruses that are unhinged and out of control, but their brains that are "unstable" and "dysregulated." Incestuously abused women diagnosed with PTSD suffer from irrational and "distorted belief structures," their amygdalae become "dysregulated" and "disorganized." They "get overwhelmed" and lose control of their psychic conflicts. As Hippocrates wrote of uteruses, their amygdalae create chaos in their bodies and minds; they break down and violate their own order of health, becoming, in effect, hysterical. Or, as contemporary trauma researcher M. Harvey notes, eerily suggesting Melampus, these women "have symptoms instead of memories": they are not oppressed by a political system that permits the sexual violation of girl children in families and uses sexual violence to control and discipline girls and women, but are disordered by an intractability within.

Do these words matter? Of course they do, because they underpin an idiom that effectively acts to keep women cordoned off in the land of the irrational, the constitutionally hysterical, the conditionally legitimate. The not qualified. The deviant.

To put things the other way round, the medical profession's time-worn determination to use gender to mark the difference between the sane and the insane, the rational and the irrational, the doctor and the patient, rational men and uncontrollable women is not only about salvaging the millennia-old idea of a natural link between women and madness, although some, including myself, would say that's part of it. It's also about power. By determinedly continuing to come up with new theories that "prove" that women's unruly bodies are to blame for their psychic discontent, the medical profession simultaneously incorporates its female patients into an age-old political and social genealogy of power, one that legitimates men's right to succession and politically castrates women. Underneath all the theorizing are ideas about continuity, authority, and the right to rule, about who gets to call the shots and who doesn't, who gets to set the terms of the debate, who gets to call what's foul and what's fair, who gets to impute deviance to whom, who gets locked up and who doesn't.

Let's not overstate the case. When the idea of incest as trauma and the diagnosis of PTSD were introduced as a way of understanding incest and remediating incest's harmful consequences, it did, at least for a moment, bring attention to and increase social awareness of the prevalence of incest and the damage it caused. It also paved the way for reparations to be paid in the form of insurance reimbursements and possible legal suits. By offering incestuously abused girls and women conceptual tools and a vocabulary through which they could begin to lend meaning to their distressing experiences, talk therapy offered hope to tens of millions of girls and women who, like Augustine, had always been dismissed or told that they "made it all up." And it imputed to those painful and distressing experiences a seriousness that warranted consideration. That in itself—taking incestuously abused women seriously—was a radical political move and critically important to identifying

22. In this MAGA rally poster, Democratic presidential candidate Hillary Clinton looks as exasperated as do many of the girls incarcerated at the Kansas State Industrial Farm (see illustration 8).

23. It's not just incestuously abused women, but all women who deviate from normative gender rules who risk being pathologized by the custodians of labels in the medical profession. In 1992, when Anita Hill charged Clarence Thomas with sexual harassment, she was diagnosed with erotomania, nymphomania, and the newly minted "victimization disorder," implying that she was delusional. No one expressed concerns about Thomas's mental state.

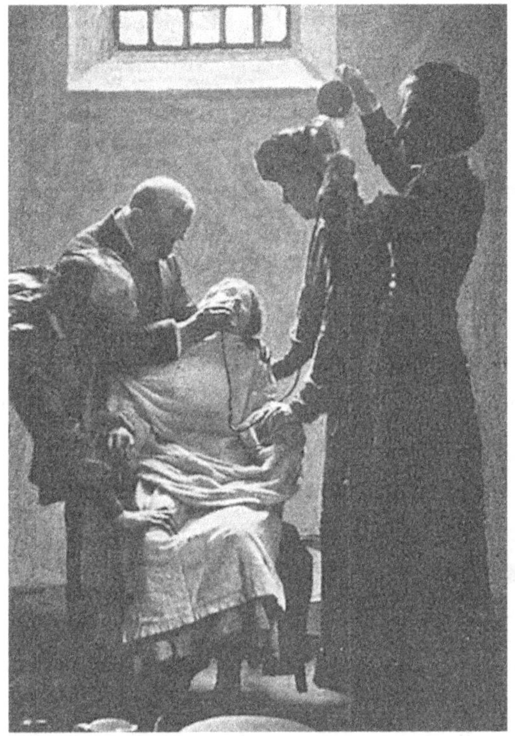

24. Noted suffragist Pleasance Pendred was imprisoned in 1913 after breaking windows in London government office buildings. After a hunger strike that lasted about two months, she was force-fed, a common treatment for discontented and suffering women incarcerated in madhouses and asylums of the time, suggesting that resistance to listening to women's concerns was widespread across a range of male-dominated institutions.

incest as a crime that deserved both social and medical consideration.

What I'm underscoring here, though, is that the link the psychiatric establishment continues to rely on between women's "innate" biological sensitivity and their tendency to psychic distress is not unique. Rather, it's just one more example of a millennia-old tradition of genderizing behavior and theorizing gendered behavior to which we are still directly or indirectly heirs. Going forward, we need to think about how cultural myths about women's inherent deficiencies, weaknesses, and mental disorders might influence the evolution of different iterations of trauma theory and the psychiatric profession's ideas about how to best treat women who have been injured by incest and other forms of heterosexist sexual violence.

Recently, we've seen some indication that a few medical professionals are attempting to become more aware of and wrestle with the profession's wholesale and long-standing reliance on the gendered truths of the past. Yet it remains the fact that the fundamental traditions of the conversation about women and mental instability, the underlying assumptions, still lie very much in the shadow of ancient Greek thinking. The very modern idea of PTSD with its emphasis on the disorder within goes back directly to the 4th and 5th centuries BCE and Hippocrates's *Diseases of Women*. As Melampus argued, the virgins' flight, their resistance to patriarchal subordination, was an "illness," a disorder of the uterus, not a meaningful response to subordination itself. And we need to keep in mind that even well-intentioned scientists and physicians (and there *are* some) working now to parse and find differently nuanced versions of PTSD were brought up on exactly those classical ideas, prejudices, and slogans that I have been addressing. Again, I'm not suggesting that we are mere victims of our cultural inheritance. But ancient medical myths and traditions have had a much greater impact than we want to acknowledge on our present-day medical conventions and assumptions, and on deciding how women's bodily and psychic distress might best be managed. And gender and concerns about preserving unequal structures of power have obviously been an important part of that mix.

It takes but a quick glance at contemporary psychiatric literature to realize that we're at an especially critical moment as the psychiatric profession increasingly turns to neurobiological studies to validate its theories and support new treatment options for women who have experienced incest and other forms of sexual violence.

Scientists have been weighing and measuring women's brains and finding them short for centuries. Over time, the so-called "female" brain has been mocked and lambasted for being underdeveloped, undersized, evolutionarily inferior, and poorly wired—and those "facts" have been cited as legitimate evidence for keeping women out of positions of power and influence.

Take the technology that has captured neuroscientists' hearts, the fMRI machine. Because brain scans are putatively free of bias, it's just as easy to assign objectivity and truth value to fMRI scans as it was to Charcot's campy medical porn, no matter how ridiculous or preposterous the interpretation of the evidence or how overtly ideological. Women's much-vaunted—and exploited—multitasking strengths? A matter of their larger and wider "corpus callosum highways." Men's genius for math and science? A matter of their more coolly logical left hemispheres and their mind-bogglingly efficient "callosal filtering abilities."

There are many problems here, not the least of which is the still uncertain relationship between the size or weight of any brain structure and the expression of a behavior. There's also the concern faced by Charcot and the scientists and physicians involved in the gonorrhea epidemics about what data ought to be collected and what might be ignored, how to scrub the data collected—"clean" is the more commonly used euphemism for determining what's relevant and what's not ("Get rid of the snake … in your pants … It's a sin")—, how to smooth anatomical differences, and how to warp brain characteristics to suit the template being used. And then we've always got to be aware of who's interpreting the data produced.

But even putting aside those fundamental questions, we can already see how these new data are being used to justify essentialist notions about women and

25. In 2011, when Christine Lagarde was appointed managing director and chairman [*sic*] of the International Monetary Fund, it was widely suggested that her biologically based linguistic skills and her feminine ability to spot emotional undertones in conversation would give her a much-needed leg up in the male-dominated world of global finance.

26. Published reports indicating that women's innate deficiencies in math kept them from occupations in STEM professions must have been music to former Harvard president Larry Summers's ears after he came under fire in 2005 for publicly declaring that "issues of intrinsic aptitude" kept women from top positions in science and math.

mental illness in a way that supports and reinforces gender stereotypes while insidiously legitimizing ideas about men's right to positions of leadership and power and women's innate inferiority. Neuroscientists, for example, recently reported that women experience depression and anxiety twice as much as men because they are biologically more vulnerable to mental distress. Canadian researcher Paul R. Albert, for example, asserts that depression in women can be attributed to "biological sex differences," not "confounding social and economic factors." Others argue that women have less adaptive coping mechanisms than men and therefore are more susceptible to emotional wounding. Other studies indicate that "abnormalities" in the amygdala, hippocampus, and medial frontal cortex of women who have experienced incest (and other forms of sexual violence) potentially reprise traditional notions about women's special susceptibility to damage and even brain-based hysteria: researchers have questioned if the "smaller intracranial volume (brain size)," "lower IQs," "poorer grades," and "increase in global atrophy" shown are due to the effects of trauma or are the result of a preexisting neurological vulnerability.

My point here is not that we ought to be wary of neuroscience, although I think we should be very wary of how neuroscience might be used by scientists, medical professionals, mainstream traumatologists, and the media to undermine the injurious impact of incest and to support conventional sexist notions of biological difference and women's innate susceptibility to madness. Neuroscientific studies of women who've experienced incest and been diagnosed with PTSD may have some utility going forward in helping us understand the psychological and physiological impact of incest. But I think we have to be very alert to who determines the concepts of normality and deviance underlying these studies and to how that data might be tricked out for political purposes as was done when women were barred from the space program.

There is no reason to think that these current studies or their interpretations are any less susceptible to ideological pressures and prejudicial attitudes than were Charcot's photographs or the results of the Gram stains that were used to identify gonorrhea in young girls during the nationwide epidemics of the 19th and first half of the 20th centuries. And I don't think it's too far-fetched in the Trump-MAGA era to see that many of the traditions that I have been highlighting are re-emerging again and again. Let's not forget that we are only a few decades removed from a time when dissatisfied and psychologically distressed women were coercively lobotomized and subjected to electric shock therapy to enforce passivity and muteness. Today, similar impulses persist: The recent overturning of *Roe v. Wade* is a stark reminder that control over women's bodies is far from a relic of the past. Almost every day, we hear some intransigent misogynist such as US congressional

27. Initially, women were not allowed to participate in the US space program, as it was generally agreed that it would be imprudent to permit people whose reasoning abilities were compromised by their "raging hormones" on board spacecraft.

representative Brad Tschida insisting that a woman's uterus has "no specific purpose to her life or well-being" (instead, it is strictly a "sanctuary" set aside for another person). And many state legislatures have passed laws that criminalize abortion with few or no exceptions for minors, even in cases of incest and rape. Given historical and present realities, it's not unreasonable to think that neuroscientific studies could be used politically as was done during the eugenics era, a movement promoting selective breeding, when policymakers weaponized intelligence measures, such as the Stanford Revision of the Binet-Simon IQ test (the progenitor of today's discriminatory Scholastic Aptitude Test [SAT]) to humiliate, quarantine, and surgically impose ideology on women who have experienced incestuous abuse.

We have much to be thankful for. The psychiatric management of the mental distress caused by incest has had some benefits and, to a degree, has rid itself of some of the misogynistic ideas that led to the brutal and punitive treatments of the past. Recent therapeutic and pharmacological treatments for women who have experienced incest (and other forms of sexual violence) have enabled many women to live more comfortable lives and have kept many women damaged by incest from incarceration in jails or psychiatric hospitals. But before we embrace any new diagnostic terms or neurobiologically based theories of trauma, we need to think more about how they might be used to trivialize incest and to underscore and reassert cultural myths

28. After being incestuously assaulted, Carrie Buck was deemed "feeble-minded," despite her good grades at school. After giving birth to the child produced by the incest, she was forcibly sterilized in 1927. Might today's neuroscientific claims of the "defective" brains of other daughters who have experienced incest be used to resuscitate the eugenics era's "Moron Girl"?

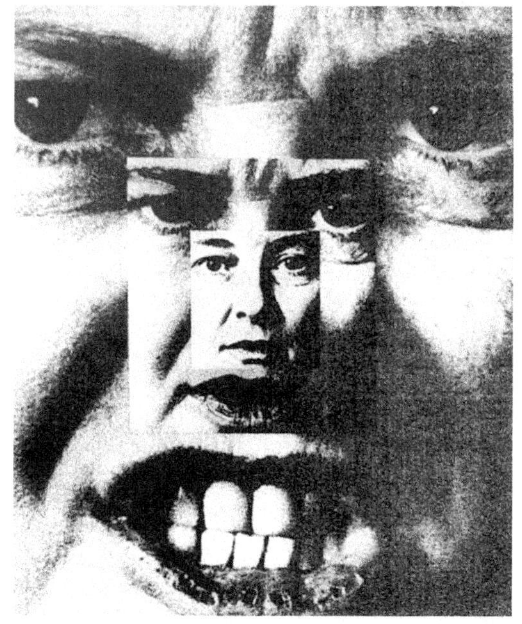

29. Pharmaceutical companies have long used science to help enforce and preserve social norms. In this 1965 ad, the tranquilizer Valium was promoted as a way of taming the anxiety, depression, and stubbornness of feminist women.

30. In his best-selling book, *The Body Keeps the Score*, psychiatrist Bessel van der Kolk writes that "child abuse ... is the single most preventable cause of mental illness." Such blithe, casual indifference to the causal complexities of incest just won't do.

about women, mental illness, and conventional gender differences. What I mean is that when we think about theories and diagnoses and the overrepresentation of women in the psychiatric system, we have to look beyond the overconfident, self-promoting, politically naive generalizations that emerge from the mouths of lionized members of the psychiatric community.

Put differently, before buying into the seductively phrased offerings of the multibillion-dollar health industry, we need to stop and think more about how any treatment offered might enforce women's historic role as in-valids or "patients" and serve to support traditional relations of dominance and subservience more generally.

We also need to start thinking beyond healing and surviving, as important as these are. Instead, we must focus more on the fundamental structures of power and inbuilt prejudices that got us here in the first place. Incest has long been treated as a private matter, but in truth, it is a profound social injustice—one that affects us all and demands our collective attention. Going forward, we need to think a lot more and a lot harder about how "facts" about women and mental illness are conceptualized, organized, and legitimized in a situation that is already unjust, in part by being vigilant to the ways that the medical and psychiatric establishments might—will?—continue to channel women's unhappiness, suffering, and anger into categories of deviance. It's also important that we ask ourselves why this model of womanhood, the inherently unstable woman, remains

31. Medically minded critics diagnosed Alex in *Fatal Attraction* with borderline personality disorder, a 20th-century redo of hysteria, and "erotomania" (the same form of hysteria that felled poor Ophelia and nearly derailed Anita Hill). It's probably unnecessary to note Alex's bedhead hair and off-the-shoulder gown. Notably, as with Clarence Thomas, the mental state of Dan, the film's male lead, went unremarked. In 1987, the year of the movie's release, it was the highest-grossing film in the world.

even now a normalized cultural symbol as well as an appealing model for the psychiatric profession.

I'm certainly not suggesting that all psychiatric professionals and neuroscientists are misogynists or sexists. But what I am suggesting is that the stereotypical model of the disaffected and unhappy woman as a "disordered patient" is tolerated by many in and outside the medical community because it has no power to effect threatening cultural change. I'm not saying incest does not cause real psychic and physiological harm; *it does profoundly disturb a girl's bodily integrity and her sense of self and being in the world.* But it is much safer for the patriarchal order to encourage and allow unhappy and suffering women to express their grievances and discontent through idioms of illness than to have them agitate for political, legal, and economic rights. Perhaps that is why the medical model of incest has remained so popular: it does nothing to transform the imbalance of gender and power. Instead, it shifts attention away from the misogynistic and sexist social and political context in which incest occurs and makes the work of remediating incest the daughter's responsibility. As such, it turns the aftermath of the sexual violence into a disorder and the incestuous behavior into a mere preceding event. As a result, it eclipses the father from our view as successfully as the refashioning of the etiology of gonorrhea and Charcot's deafness to Augustine's words.

PART 4

Incest, Sexual Violence, and
the Politics of Shame

TO BETTER ILLUSTRATE HOW institutional power constructs and structures female shame, I'd like to begin with the Bible and the story of Genesis.

Genesis, the first book of the Old Testament, is usually read as a sweeping account of origins. It tells the story of the creation of the world, the early history of humanity, and the ancestry of the Jewish people. But it is just as much a story about patriarchal power, the social and political value of heterosexist sexual violence, and the shaming of girls and women.

Genesis 34, for instance, begins when Dinah, about age twelve, sets off by herself to see local women preparing for a special occasion. Prince Shechem spots her, rapes her, and rides off into the rest of the narrative to engage in high-level mediations about law and governance. Dinah's story stops there. In the thirty to eighty words it costs to tell her history, she never speaks—nor does any woman in Genesis—and after the prince sexually attacks her, she is only referred to as a utility to consolidate male power.

32. Perhaps for fear of censure, James Tissot made his Dinah look anything but the child she was when raped. In some versions of this story, Dinah, as here, is kidnapped and raped by multiple men, which only makes this story sadder, and more disturbing.

There's something refreshingly direct about the no-frills way Dinah's story is told. No setting, no dialogue, no turning point moment or *denouement*; not a word about what she was wearing. But what especially interests me about this classic moment of sexual violence is its entanglement with shame. The smut's all his, but the blameless target of his violence is tainted with the prince's shame and dishonor. The word the Old Testament authors use to represent the rape, *innah*, is significant too. Shechem *innahed* her, a Hebrew word that in its verb form denotes not just rape but also status degradation, a lowering of rank. In other words, Shechem doesn't just violently assault Dinah; he also bows her down, he lowers her social status; his actions induct her into a lower realm. She is now an outsider, a less than, at least according to the socially and institutionally accepted ideological values and practices of masculinist culture. His rape spoils her identity and indicates permanent and unremitting failure. As later medieval commentators noted, Dinah lived the rest of her life in a state of "corruption, a state of harlotry."

Classic victim shaming? To be sure. But if we want to better understand—and do something about—victim shaming, we need to start by thinking more fundamentally about shame itself. What is shame and what is its purpose? How has it been defined, and how does it work according to those who've defined it? How do powerful institutional structures and political forces continue to engender female shame, and who benefits from the perpetuation of such shaming?

To answer those questions, we first need to clear away some historical debris.

Since earliest times, philosophers have conceived of shame as a generic, gender-neutral emotion, an affective inheritance that belongs to each of us equally. "Shame is an originary [original and natural] experience," explains noted American philosopher Anthony Steinbock, citing the work of his esteemed predecessor, Max Scheler. Shame has nothing to do with power or history, so these eminent thinkers tell us; rather, it is a generalized condition of dishonor, an emotion experienced when we fail to live up to our values or ideals. Echoing their predecessors, contemporary philosophers John Rawls and Dan Zahavi explain that we experience shame when we fail to achieve certain excellences. I feel shame when I betray my values. We feel shame when we fail to be the sort of people we want to be. "Rather than being inherently debilitating, shame … play[s] a constructive role in moral development" because it can "motivate me to reorient my way of living," instructs Zahavi. Shame's purpose? Self-improvement and redemption, an often painful knock upside the head reminding us to make sure we're living up to our ideals. Ultimately, shame pushes us toward higher dimensions of human existence.

When feminists express their concerns about these myopic generalizations, their "gender biases," as they are generally referred to, are dismissed as curious side

33. To say that philosophy's work remains embedded in the masculinist enterprise is almost too obvious to write. When MIT professor Sally Haslanger was in graduate school (1979–1985), a faculty member told her that he had "never seen a first-rate woman philosopher and never expected to because women were incapable of having seminal ideas." After she earned a distinction on her preliminary exams, the department suggested that she undergo a blood test to determine if she was "really a woman."

problems, irreverent and certainly irritating at times, but nothing that warrants much consideration. Even if philosophers sometimes cringe at the ridiculousness of it all, generally they think that all this kvetching and pissing and moaning is okay. And the reason they think it's okay is that they do not think it matters very much.

There is a luxurious and rank narcissism reflected in philosophy's complacent repudiation of ideas that lie beyond the orbit of its narrow ken. As past and present philosophers have it, the specifics of shame, shame's entanglement with a person's social position, privilege, and experiences, are simply not part of the calculus. Missing from all this heady thinking is any recognition of how most women experience shame—women like the 81 percent of American women who have experienced some form of sexual assault, women like Dinah who was raped as a child, women like those tens of millions who have experienced incestuous violence. It's the *innah* thing they don't seem to get, or don't want to get. Or maybe they just find the use of sexual violence to enforce social stratification and reproduce systems of domination and subordination inconsequential. A woman's concern.

Of course, preserving patriarchal authority, which is really what all this shaming comes down to, doesn't start with a girl's first experience of sexual violence. Rather, it begins the day she is born. Like an investiture ceremony, once a child is assigned the female gender according to the institutionally recommended standards of preference,

34. Thomas Aquinas, patron saint of academics, philosophers, students, and publishers, was also a great propagandist for masculinist traditions. Because women are born "defective and misbegotten," he explained, when Eve ate the apple, she only confirmed her natural shame status.

certain licenses and privileges are subtracted from her and conferred onto the "boy." As a female, the girl child is no longer a member of "generic" humanity: she has been ritually separated from her place in the legitimate order. She's now outside it. Very quickly, girls learn that they are shamed subjects of The Look, the male gaze, while boys' bodies remain relatively invisible insofar as they can more easily evade the threat of being seen, objectified, and targeted by others. Put differently, our gendered bodies place us either in the position of having the power to shame or to be seen as shameful.

The point here is simple but important. For girls and women, shame is not always the result of a moral oopsie. Rather, shame comes with the female gender. Shechem's rape simply cements Dinah into her rightful shame status.

We see all of this easy indifference writ large when we consider incest and its special shame, commonly referred to as its "ick factor." "[T]here [is] 'definitely an ick factor,'" noted Stephen Bainbridge, a UCLA law professor, in 2011 when asked to comment on the ethics of a prominent professor's incestuous abuse of his daughter, and this ick factor produces a different uneasiness than we might feel when thinking or talking about rape or sexual harassment. Incest's ickiness, its legendary powers of contamination and outsized reputation for infectiousness, were seen in especially high relief during the 1980s and 1990s following the publication of Judith Lewis Herman's and Lisa Hirschman's groundbreaking clinical and cultural examination of incest, *Father-Daughter Incest*, and the unprecedented publication of various types of incest narratives, a novelty that troubled a number of typically unflappable male critics and academics. "One of the most frightening aspects of our new interest in, and knowledge of, intrafamilial sex," explained former University of Florida professor and innovative logician James Twitchell, "is that the incidence of incest *seems* to be increasing exponentially as information becomes available … [I]f incestuous behavior is a learned process, a communicable disease as some social scientists now assert with reference to the undeniable explosions in statistics, then this may well turn out to be a major public health problem for which the only cure may be … its return to obscurity and silence." Unlike rape and other forms of sexual violence against women, incest's contagious quality seems to elicit a surprising germaphobia, even among our most eminent philosophers.

For example, in response to the same publishing phenomenon, award-winning philosopher Ian Hacking, professor emeritus at the University of Toronto, put out this uncharacteristic bit of fretting: " … some of the increase in child abuse [*sic*] is due to the publicity itself, in that it makes available new descriptions under which to act, and then, by semantic contagion, leads on to yet worse actions." We hear almost a kind of eugenicist's anxiety in these scholars' concerns. Unlike other forms of sexual violence, according to these savants, incest seems to possess such rare and astounding properties of infectivity that, like the microbes responsible for avian flu, they have the ability to cross species from literature to real life where they will infect and apparently spawn new forms of sexual impurity and violence. Even naming incest, so Hacking implies, would constitute a dangerous trespass and could well hurtle us into a monstrous place devoid of reason and morality.

Of course, there's more here than just a thinly veiled appeal to incest's mythological dangers and a grim warning that we will descend into some inchoate and apocalyptic un-zone, a moral no zone, if girls and women even speak the word incest. Break down Hacking's stern caution to its most common denominator and what we discover is simply a gussied-up way of telling girls and women who have been oppressed by incest to just shut up and stop rocking the boat.

So just what does drive our culture's persistent and tenacious determination to suppress incest? Many things I suspect. When I'm feeling charitable, I think a bit comes from a desire felt by some living in the Trump 2.0 era that we just go back to "the way things were," and that way includes keeping "not nice" topics out of the public discourse. An old-fashioned sense of prudery might account for some of the silence that surrounds incest. But I suspect that's not very much. I do feel quite certain that a lot comes from a wish shared by many that gobby women would just put up and shut up and stop nattering on about the bullies in the playground. But the more I look at the suppression techniques used now and in the past, the more they seem to fit the patterns of systemic oppression that I have been writing about.

Male culture's determination to conceal all evidence of incest is not just about subordinating girls and women and securing gender stratification, although that does account for a great deal of it. It's not just about learned behavior either. Instead, the suppression of incest, past and present, has to do with power and doing whatever it takes to preserve patriarchal ideology and all its allowances as the dominant ideology in the West.

During the mid-19th century and the first half of the 20th, girls' gonorrhea infections directly incriminated their fathers. Had their fathers' abuse of power been exposed, it would have presented a serious challenge to the ideology of male supremacy. The emperors, in other words, would have been seen without their clothes on, and instead of virtuous patriarchs, all we would have seen were entitled fathers and criminals. But it's not just the fathers who would have been shown to be naked. The Father would have been revealed, the entire patriarchal system that permits fathers' tacit sexual right to their daughters would have been exposed as a lie, morally bankrupt, debauched. Ironically, in the early 20th century, when White House officials declared infected girls a threat to the nation-state, they were dead on. The gonorrhea epidemics did threaten society with social dissolution. Their existence and the potential exposure of the fathers' transgressions quite literally threatened the nation-state with non-structure. Incest had to be suppressed. Revelation that incest was—and is—ubiquitous would have had a tornadic effect. It would have ripped the roof off the house.

Put bluntly, the revelation that incest is not an aberration but rather endemic, an inevitable outgrowth of patriarchal culture, would undo many people's places in existence. It would upend all the truths they hold dear about themselves and the system that ensures their entitlements and their impunity.

And for many, just the idea of that is really very scary.

One last word. The shaming of girls and women is embedded in the structures of patriarchy. It pervades our language, our medical practices, and our policies.

As I've noted, shame is a powerful tool for enforcing and reinforcing social norms, operating as a systemic form of control that predates any individual experience of sexual violence. Its silencing effect prevents women from recognizing that the violence they have endured is not isolated but part of a larger pattern. By discouraging disclosure and solidarity, shame helps maintain fathers' implicit sexual ownership of their daughters and gender stratification. As such, the shaming of girls and women who have experienced incest and other forms of sexual violence relentlessly reinstates and legitimizes social injustice.

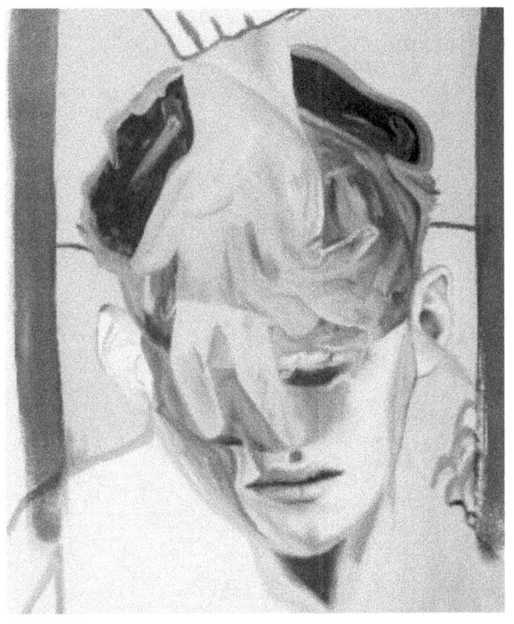

35. Shame can destroy the lifeworlds of girls who have experienced incestuous violence; it is often experienced as a sense of oppressive, intolerable degradation.

Some, including myself, have argued that the shaming of women makes male supremacy resilient beyond its ability to secure its own formal institutionalization in law and policy. If this is true—and I believe that it is—then better understanding the politics of shame is essential to understanding how to expose the suppression of incest.

And that means we have work to do.

PART 5

Where Do We Go from Here?

SO MUCH FOR THE problem. Now how do we fix it?

Like many women, I wish I knew. There can't be a woman anywhere who has experienced incest who hasn't wondered what to do about what's been done without courting further abuse and possibly upending her family's social and financial security. We know that some women have spoken out and successfully gained widespread media attention: in recent years, most visibly Dylan Farrow. BBC England picked up the story of Poppy, an eighteen-year-old English woman who, in 2023, publicly disclosed details of her grandfather's incestuous attacks against her when she was a prepubescent girl. And in 2024, Hadley Duvall—a young woman whose stepfather incestuously assaulted her—caught the spotlight for a minute when she was pressed into service by the Democratic National Committee to highlight its case for abortion rights during their national convention in August. But a few women catching the eye of the press is not going to change things.

More speak-outs? Not going to work. Nor will girl-power campaigns, more money for social service agencies, local or institutional mandates requiring medical and other professionals to report evidence of incest, extending statute of limitation laws, and discouraging malicious defamation suits as was done recently in New Jersey, New York, and California. Not even women-centered, strengths-based psychotherapies and mindfulness techniques—as much as they may provide some relief—go far enough to upend the entrenched and intersecting systems of power that keep incest invisible. The big issues I have been considering here are not going to be solved by teaching judo to young girls or by creating watchdog agencies tasked with ensuring that the government and the medical and legal professions' status and ideology of ethicality don't become a mask for privilege, power, prejudice, and suppression rather than—as is so often claimed—modes of advancing women's well-being.

So what can we do?

Vote more women into public office in the hope that they will lobby for new legislation? Excellent idea, but I don't think even that's going to bring about the change we need. After all, the Violence Against Women Act was passed in 1994 (and reauthorized in 2022), but that hasn't put a dent in the number of girls and young women who experience incest and other forms of sexualized male violence. Improve the economic rights of women so that no mother needs to stay with a partner who is sexually assaulting a daughter (or daughters)? Incrementally, we have done that in the form of laws such as the Lilly Ledbetter Fair Pay Act of 2009, the Equal Pay Act of 1963, the Family and Medical Leave Act of 1993, and statewide policies and initiatives such as the Women's Economic Empowerment Initiative. All of these practical efforts are valuable and enabling, but they work to erode only part of the larger social and institutional systems that sustain incest.

Another radical social movement such as we saw emerge during the early 1970s? Maybe, possibly, a little. Without a sustained, decades-long feminist social movement, a.k.a. a lay referral service, the recognition that the psychic distresses caused by incest were not fantasies but were caused by fathers' criminal behaviors might never have occurred. However, if we reflect on the recent successes of #MeToo—and they have been considerable—we have to admit that they haven't made a blind bit of difference where incest is concerned. Even the well-respected attempts by Judith Herman and other feminist psychiatric professionals to bring attention to the injurious impact of incest and the political context in which incest occurs have failed to upset the unequal structures of power that keep us from disrupting the father's sense of impunity and his tacit entitlement to his daughters. Nor have these efforts reduced the number of girls who continue to be subjugated by incest.

Patience? Although gradual change will almost certainly take place, given that laws criminalizing domestic violence were only codified thirty years ago, and that the medical profession only begrudgingly began to accept that the injuries caused by incest were not just another expression of women's natural hysterical makeup at about the same time, if I'm right about the deep political, social, and institutional structures that enable the continual sexual oppression of daughters by fathers (and father surrogates), gradualism will take far too long, for me at least.

The bottom line is this: If we want to do something about incest, we have to change the way we see and talk about incest, and that means we have to put fathers back in the picture. And that's not going to be easy. A few years ago, Legal Momentum, a legal advocacy organization for women, came up with a list of witty sexual assault prevention tips for men "Guaranteed To Work!" The tips include "Don't put drugs in people's drinks in order to control their behavior," "Remember, people go into the laundry to do their laundry, do not attempt to molest someone who is alone in a laundry room," "If you are in an elevator and someone else gets in, DON'T ASSAULT [HER]," and "USE THE BUDDY SYSTEM! If you are not able to stop yourself from assaulting people, ask a friend to stay with you while you are in public." They're good for a giggle; they're sly and they poke a bit of gentle fun at men's sense of sexual entitlement. But part of the reason we laugh is because it's absurd to think of any of these strategies being enacted or enforced, or for us to imagine that any such strategies could be enforced. And they become downright preposterous if we apply them to fathers. "If you think you can't resist sexually assaulting your daughter when you enter her bedroom, take a buddy with you!" And this points to one of the most challenging obstacles to our seeing incest: To reduce or eliminate incest, we have to reconsider the ways that we provide fathers with protection from scrutiny, and there we butt up against a core tenet of democratic society: When we try to limit the power of the family head, we encounter the fundamental tension between civil liberties and social control.

So, no oversight committees for dads? I don't think so. But that leaves us nowhere as well, and that's not acceptable.

What, then, could we do to make us all more aware of the prevalence and reality of incest and stop it?

Possibly a few things. First, when representing and writing about incest (and other forms of sexual violence against girls and women), it's crucial that we emphasize the systemic nature of the problem. To do so, we need to reconsider our conventional way of talking about incest. I'm referring to the story that we all know so well, the sensationalized one that focuses on the weak, damaged, and suffering girl—who has typically been told that she lies—and occasionally a cop or more likely a therapist playing a bit part as a kind of *deus ex machina*, the all-too-familiar account that portrays incest as a rare event, an atypical moment of sadistic, sexualized violence that typically occurs in out-of-the-way places most of us have never heard of. Instead, we need to frame incest for what it truly is: not a surprising anomaly, a rare breakdown of the social order, but a common event that forms part of patriarchy's normal social baseline, like racism.

Because modern patriarchal culture has framed incest as a medical issue rather than a form of political oppression, we might also try thinking differently about women's psychic distress. Not as a state of wellness or ill health, but rather as impasse—a predicament or perhaps better, a deadlock, a socially mediated experience that affords no obvious escape, self-affirmation, or protest. Let me explain. When medicine is faulted, it is typically for its technical limitations and rarely because it excludes the social causes of ailments. Once an incestuously abused woman enters the medical system, the social and political aspects of her history disappear behind labels such as "dissociative disorder," "trauma," "interpersonal violence," and "adverse childhood experiences" (ACEs). Although wonderfully scientificky-sounding, these gender-neutral and anodyne terms isolate the girls and women from the social and political context that permits the crime, and hide the fathers who commit the crimes just as successfully as not naming them at all. So, a question: How might our understanding of women's distress evolve if we reframe our perspective and view women who have experienced incestuous abuse not solely as isolated individuals with distinct psychological and physical experiences, but also as members of a larger entity—specifically, the body of all women subjected to systemic sexual oppression?

It might also be fruitful if we started to challenge the dualistic assumptions (body/mind, sick/not sick, sane/insane, private/public, etc.) that ground the psychiatric profession's deterministic theories and treatment plans in a way that might reveal their prejudices, conflicts, and paradoxes. For example, if we agree that the mind is not simply a biological organ but a social construct, where does that leave us when trying to find more just forms of understanding and dealing with women's psychic distress? We might also ask ourselves if any psychiatric treatment free of engagement with the social and political context in which the sexual violence occurs should continue to be the cornerstone of remedial work, especially with women who experience the highest proportion of sexual violence—incest—or whether politically decontextualized work is simply another form of oppression.

But it's not just more thoughtful and nuanced medical theory and practice that we need. We also need to look at the long-standing sexist and misogynistic rhetorical and linguistic tactics and strategies the medical establishment and other male-dominated institutions use every day to codify and talk about those ideas. I'm not suggesting that we revisit the language property debates of the '70s and '80s. It's been long understood that men, primarily white men, have held nearly exclusive tenancy on the English language since its emergence (despite some recent memorable incursions by women, "mansplaining" being one of the more delightful ones) and still do: A physician should consider testing for STIs if "[t]he child has a sibling, other relative, or another person in the household with an STI." Certainly, we've made a bit of progress since the dark days of 2020 when the vaunted *Oxford English Dictionary* (*OED*) engaged in a hasty PR campaign to recover its integrity and reputation for neutrality after it came to light that the words "wench" and "piece" were still offered as synonyms for "woman."

But my hunch is that if we're going to make any real progress, we need to look harder at the ways not just medical language but our ordinary language remains as intimately intertwined with ideology and gender hierarchies as is the psychiatric profession's vernacular, and reinforces the radical separation we've seen since the beginning of Western medicine between women and reason, legitimacy, and authority. If we do that, even on a cursory level, we see that even in our most respected dictionaries, including *Merriam-Webster* and the now hopefully woke *OED*, women remain the defining example for the disordered, the disarranged, the crazy— the not qualified. Not convinced? Try googling "define disordered." The first definition offered, from the now (supposedly) progressive group at Oxford Languages, reads "not neatly arranged; confused and untidy," and the primary example of the word's use reads, "She went to comb her disordered hair." Honestly, they might have

36. After the *OED*'s comeuppance, other dictionaries, including Italy's prestigious *Treccani*, rushed to eliminate their own "wenches," "whores," "bits," "birds," and "bitches."

just saved themselves the bother of writing an example sentence and simply written "see woman; nuts." Still not convinced? Try playing the dictionary game yourself; google the definition of "hysteria" and synonyms for "hysteria" on the *Merriam-Webster* dictionary website where you will find among the list of synonyms "disorder," "delirium," "chaos," and "rampage." The only example of "hysteria" that allows for synonym substitution reads: "the *hysteria* of the mother when she realized that she had lost her four-year-old son in the crowd." In this age of "negger," "hepeating," and the Brits' marvelous "handbagging," it may take a minute for the tenacity of heterosexist definitions to sink in, but if you are ever doubtful about the extent to which women's exclusion from reason and legitimacy is still deeply embedded in our culture, I offer you "disorder" and "hysteria."

Yet it's not just the words that we *do* use but the ones we don't use that just as clearly reveal long-standing and powerful ideological and misogynistic prejudices, and contribute to our inability to see incest. Take the word "rapist," for example. Or "sexual harasser." Both of these names identify the perpetrator of a crime of sexual violence. Harvey Weinstein is a rapist; he raped. Andrew Cuomo is a sexual harasser; he sexually harassed. Jeffrey Epstein was a sex trafficker; he trafficked. But what is the name for the father who sexually exploits his daughter(s) for years? We have none. And that's the point. Linguistically speaking, he doesn't exist.

37. When women are called hysterical, as happened to then-Senator Kamala Harris after she questioned the former US Attorney General Jeff Sessions in 2017, it underpins an idiom that serves to remove the authority and force of what women have to say and brings with it all the loaded connotations of disorder and irrationality that have always accompanied the word.

Does this absence matter? Of course it does, because it helps maintain our culture's long-cherished and deeply held ideas about the innocence, virtue, and moral superiority of fathers. Not naming him eclipses him and decouples him from any suspicion of criminal behavior. The absence harbors and abets a criminal. We don't even have a verb to describe his behavior. Weinstein raped. Cuomo harassed. Epstein trafficked. But what did the father do? Right now, we have no way of distinguishing the way his behavior differs from that of any other sexual violence criminal's. So let me suggest that we start naming the perpetrator of incest as an "incestor" and using a verb that names what he did: He "incested." "The allegation made by Dylan Farrow against the *incestor* she names—her father, Woody Allen—has been described by journalists and industry figures as very compelling." "Ronan Farrow, Dylan's brother, has publicly stated that he unequivocally supports her allegation that the person she names *incested* her."

It's worth pausing a minute to press home the significance of this omission. We all know that the language we use was created to represent the needs and desires of the culture's epistemological stakeholders. To a great extent, the concept of "female" was discursively created by men. As decades of feminist critiques have pointed out, men have been fantasizing about women and then warping and naming their data to suit their theories throughout history. Just as Freud did when he warped and repurposed the incest narratives he had heard, just as Charcot did when he cleansed his data of Augustine's incest narrative so his findings would confirm his notion that an inner disorder, not an oppressive external act of sexual violence, caused her psychic distress. As mentioned, we also see this happening today as some neuroscientists continue to warp their data to suit long-held ideas about the innately deficient female brain.

At the risk of seeming tangential, let me come at my point a different way. I want to draw your attention to the following anatomical illustration, drawn in 1538 by the renowned anatomist Andreas Vesalius. The illustration shows the first drawing of a part of the female body, specifically its uterus, drawn by a male medical professional.

Vesalius had access to a female cadaver when drawing this image. But even with the aid of direct observation, note that the reproductive anatomy of the female is portrayed as fundamentally male. The uterus is represented as an inverted scrotal sac.

At first blush, it's hard to know what to say when confronted with such disturbing evidence of the illustrator's psychic resistance. Despite the knowledge gained from his specimen, Vesalius (and his colleagues) were unable or unwilling to see or represent a uterus and instead persisted in representing the ancient belief that a baby is born via an internal penis.

The point I'm making here is that when we only have sexist beliefs and language available to us, when

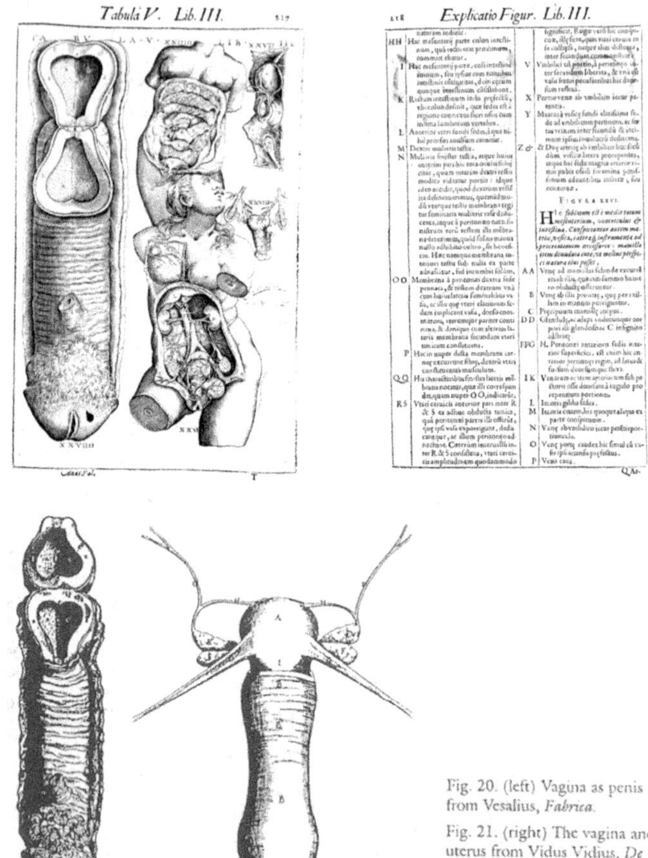

Fig. 20. (left) Vagina as penis from Vesalius, *Fabrica*.

Fig. 21. (right) The vagina and uterus from Vidus Vidius, *De anatome corporis humani* (1611)

38. A remarkable example of data cleansing.

we can only rely on the blinkered and narcissistic vision and representations of our culture's epistemological stakeholders, women and their experiences tend to be excluded and erased, often simply by omission. And so it is with incest. If we don't name it, it doesn't exist. And that is very useful to those who would like nothing better than for things to stay as they are.

Will adding a new way of using an old word to the lexicon bring an end to the practice of incest? I'm afraid not. But it may form a wee chink in the foundation of the male supremacist world, and it will certainly make it easier to talk about the foundational crime upon which heteropatriarchal culture depends.

We also need to think about the ways we might be contributing to the invisibility of incest. Even before Trump's present anti-DEI efforts, many universities and colleges closed their women's studies programs or collapsed them into gender studies programs. Some point to a lack of funding; others suggest that women's studies programs are no longer relevant, even hopelessly old-fashioned, passé, perhaps a little exclusionary. In ways, a touch elitist. The phrase "gender studies" sounds more inclusive and suggests more enlightened ideas, greater progress, and philosophical (and, with some, even moral) superiority. To be clear, I absolutely welcome the study of under-examined histories and social issues important to intersexed and LGBTQ+ peoples. That, we should all applaud. Those who have worked and continue to work to bring attention to the multiplicity and fluidity of gender should be congratulated for their sheer courage, astounding will to action, and no less astounding confidence in the possibility of change. As should those who have worked to examine cross-cultural differences in the social, familial, and institutional contexts of women who have experienced incest. But we need to remember that feminism and the formal academic study of women have always been considered a bit dodgy, self-interested, a suspect area for inquiry based on selfish and ulterior motives, not justice. If we have to eliminate any more women's studies programs, before we do, I think we'd be well-advised to consider the ways that many issues that overwhelmingly involve women—*and that includes incest*—will be given short shrift or ignored altogether. And we need to remember that the erasure of incest will be welcome news to many, not just in academic institutions. We might also ask ourselves why incest is so often relegated to an elsewhere status, even by those interested in and writing about sexual violence against women and girls. What are the costs—and who profits from—niching incest into its own prefecture instead of situating it, along with rape, sexual harassment, domestic violence, and other sexual violence crimes, on the continuum of heterosexual violence against girls and women?

If we did these things, should we be optimistic about change? Maybe. A bit. I'm struck, for example, as were many women, by the degree of public censure Woody Allen received, and what #MeToo has been able to accomplish in terms of the visibility of sexual harassment and some other forms of sexual violence against women.

But the overall picture is more bleak, I'm afraid. So far, we have not gotten anywhere near subverting the ordinary material and institutional arrangements that support and maintain incest's invisibility and its goals. None of the efforts I've mentioned here have made a blind bit of difference in upsetting the unequal structures of power that keep us from disrupting fathers' sense of entitlement to their daughters or reducing the number of girls who continue to be subjugated by incest.

So, what would it take to really do something about incest? Recognizing that the sexual coercion and exploitation of daughters is as common as research indicates would require us to radically rethink our major social and political interests, and that of course includes the family and the medical establishment. It would mean moving from local questions, including those involving individual cases of incest, and reproblematizing the whole inegalitarian, antidemocratic, and anti-feministic epistemological structure that maintains society and serves as the principal support for patriarchal ideology. What is at stake here is a question of centering, or decentering, and it involves analyzing, disrupting, and even dismantling or at least radically reconfiguring many of the material conditions and institutional structures that produce and organize society in a way that makes it unequal and unjust for beings who are constructed as women or who live as women. Put more directly, you simply can't fit women, or any aspect of women's lives, into a social structure already designed for men and male dominance and expect justice. What I'm imagining would open new possibilities, new vistas, and finally let in some air. But if we were to do this, it would require costly changes in our thinking and our institutions; society would be fundamentally upset for a time, if not permanently, and that would be deeply disruptive for us all—even for those whose privileges and self-images would not be directly threatened by eliminating incest. And my hunch is that this kind of radical decentering would be even harder for us to accept than new research findings about the coercive and cruel possibilities of fathers' sexual behaviors. After all, one reason our society has marginalized and dismissed consideration of incest is not because it is insignificant, but because its practice is so central to major social interests.

On my gloomiest days, I wonder if we're going to have to accept incest and its damage in the same way that we've had to accept war's: as a kind of collateral damage necessary for the greater good, a way of supporting the war effort so to speak. We are all so dependent on the specialized knowledge of experts in the medical profession (and others such as the legal profession) that preserve and maintain unequal structures of power that some, including myself, wonder if we could survive without it.

And so where does that leave us?

With the remarkable and insuppressible Augustine. After years of being given token rewards for maintaining decorum and respecting the madhouse's rules of good behavior—you may move out of isolation and into the public rooms, but you may only go here but not there; you may dress in street clothes today but not tomorrow—Augustine finally tore up the script. One night, she ripped the metal brackets off her cell window and escaped.

And we can all take inspiration from that.

NOTES AND FURTHER READING

The Medical Suppression of Incest (i)

p. 3 ***How come nobody talks about incest?*** **... In** this book, I define incest as any overt and intentional sexual contact (such as genital touching, masturbation, and/or oral, anal, or vaginal intercourse) between a father or surrogate, such as an older brother, uncle, grandfather, or stepfather, and a girl child that occurs in the context of a caring relationship. Incest is distinguished by its chronic, interpersonal nature; incest is not typically a single event. Unlike other sexual violence crimes against women and girls, incest typically occurs at a very young age with onset generally reported between four and nine; see Diana E. H. Russell in *The Secret Trauma: Incest in the Lives of Girls and Women* (Basic Books, 1986), 19–55, 74. While children of all genders may be incestuously abused, because incest is overwhelmingly a heterosexist crime, this book concerns itself exclusively with incest committed against daughters by fathers and father surrogates; see Howard N. Snyder, *Sexual Assault of Young Children as Reported to Law Enforcement: Victim, Incident, and Offender Characteristics* (Bureau of Justice Statistics, July 2000), https://bjs.ojp.gov/content/pub/pdf/saycrle.pdf (accessed July 7, 2025).

p. 3 *social service agencies Clorox it* … Today, incest is often euphemized by trauma researchers, therapists, and social workers as one of many adverse childhood experiences (ACEs) along with food inadequacy and discrimination; see Centers for Disease Control and Prevention, "Fast Facts: Preventing Adverse Childhood Experiences," https://www.cdc.gov/violenceprevention/aces/fastfact.html. In previous decades, child protection services often tucked incest into a box suggestively but rather unsatisfyingly labeled "Non-Accidental Injuries" (NAIs); see Linda Gordon, *Heroes of Their Own Lives: The Politics and History of Family Violence* (University of Illinois Press, 2002), 6 n. 7. The problem with these bleached-out terms, along with today's ubiquitous "child sexual abuse" (CSA), is twofold: (1) they obscure the political and social differences that distinguish incest and conduce to its occurrence and (2) they suggest gender neutrality and hide the fact that incest is not a genderless crime but overwhelmingly a heterosexist crime committed by fathers against daughters.

p. 3 *talk show hosts head for the hills* … See Ben Wattenberg, host of PBS's *Think Tank with Ben Wattenberg*, and Catharine MacKinnon, law professor at the University of Michigan and Harvard Law School, for an example of the way people duck and run for cover when the word "incest" is mentioned. Available here: https://www.youtube.com/watch?v=lW7hn-6j1Hw (PBS, July 7, 1995; accessed November 23, 2024).

p. 3 *feminists tend to leave it out* … Anita Hill's recent omission of the word "incest" when cataloging "all" forms of sexual violence on CNN's *New Day* does not, I don't think, denote any insensitivity on her part (https://transcripts.cnn.com/show/nday/date/2021-09-29/segment/04; accessed July 14, 2023). Nor does its omission by other feminists working on issues pertaining to sexual violence such as seen in Deborah Tuerkheimer's *Credible: Why We Doubt Accusers and Protect Abusers* (HarperCollins, 2021). Instead, evidence indicates that the elision speaks more to the difficulties in researching a subject deeply buried among bland and innocuously labeled categories such as ACEs and CSA, and the fear of backlash and retribution held by many feminist scholars; see Richard P. Kluft, "Ramifications of Incest," *Psychiatric Times,* January 12, 2011, https://www.psychiatrictimes.com/view/ramifications-incest) and C. A. Courtois, *Healing the Incest Wound: Adult Survivors in Therapy,* 2nd ed. (W. W. Norton & Company, 2010). On top of this, feminists know that critiquing the patriarchal nuclear family can be politically and socially perilous in our Western Christian patriarchal white supremacist society; for some, researching and writing about incest may seem very third rail.

p. 3 *Austrian monsters like Josef Fritzl* … See Matthew Weaver and Kate Connolly, "Austrian Cellar Case Man Admits Abduction and Incest," *The Guardian*, April 28, 2008 (https://www.theguardian.com/world/2008/apr/28/austria.internationalcrime2, accessed July 7, 2025) and Jian Li Zheng, "Incestuous 'Monster of Mariquita' dies in prison," *Colombia Reports,* September 16, 2011 (https://colombiareports.com/monster-of-mariquita-dies-in-prison/, accessed July 7, 2025).

p. 5 *approximately one in six* … See "Victims of Sexual Violence: Statistics," RAINN (https://www.rainn.org/statistics/victims-sexual-violence, accessed July 7, 2025).

p. 5 *conservative data indicate that* **at least** *as many American daughters experience incest before they're eighteen* … In this book, I am using what many consider the best data available: that published by Russell and by Gail Wyatt in "The Sexual Abuse of Afro-American and White Women in Childhood," *Child Abuse and Neglect* 9 (1985): 507–19. Both scholars have been praised by Judith Herman, author of the landmark *Father-Daughter Incest* (Harvard University Press, 1981; reprint 2000), for devising the "gold standard" of research methodologies. Russell and Wyatt found that incest affects girls across all socioeconomic classes and ethnic groups.

p. 5 *never reported* … See "Statistics: The Criminal Justice System," RAINN (https://rainn.org/facts-statistics-the-scope-of-the-problem/statistics-the-criminal-justice-system, accessed August 9, 2025) and Sarah Zhang, "DNA Tests Are Uncovering the True Prevalence of Incest," *The Atlantic*, March 18, 2024 (https://www.theatlantic.com/health/archive/2024/03/dna-tests-incest/677791/, accessed July 7, 2025).

p. 5 *girls under twelve* … See Snyder.

p. 7 *plenty of guys surf the net* … For an example of the way men's magazines' advice columnists reassure guys who watch incest porn, see Dave Holmes, "Am I a Creep If I Watch Incest Porn?" *Esquire*, September 29, 2016, https://www.esquire.com/lifestyle/sex/advice/a49051/ask-dave-incest-porn/ (accessed July 5, 2025).

p. 8 *Freud was not the only one writing "fairy tales"* … For more information on the suppression of Ferenczi's 1933 incest paper, "Confusion of Tongues," see Erna Olafson, David L. Corwin, and Roland C. Summit,

"Modern History of Child Sexual Abuse Awareness: Cycles of Discovery and Suppression," *Child Abuse & Neglect* 17 (1993): 7–24.

p. 9 *publishing what sounded very much like a "fairy tale."* … Freud's memory of the withering rebuke is detailed in Jeffrey Moussaieff Masson, *The Assault on Truth: Freud's Suppression of the Seduction Theory* (Pocket Books, 1998), 9–12.

p. 10 *"it is found in the fantasy encountered in most female patients—namely, that the father seduced her in childhood"* … This translation of Freud's "seduction theory" can be found in Masson, 11–12.

p. 11 *once medical technologies such as germ theory* … For basic information on infection and the history and impact of medical technologies, I have relied on standard histories of medical knowledge as well as Eliot Freidson, *Profession of Medicine: A Study of the Sociology of Applied Knowledge* (University of Chicago Press, 1988).

p. 11 *gonorrhea in girls ranked as the second most common contagious disease in the country* … For basic historical information on the epidemics, I have relied on Lynn Sacco's measured and meticulously researched *Unspeakable: Father-Daughter Incest in American History* (Johns Hopkins University Press, 2009); quotations from medical and public health professionals working during the epidemics found here: 91, 104, 138, 128, 127, 200, 98, 97, and 169. References to diversions used by physicians of the time can also be found in Suzanne M. Sgroi, "Sexual Molestation of Children: The Last Frontier in Child Abuse," *Children Today* 44 (1975): 18–21.

p. 17 ***send infected girls to reformatories*** … Nicole Perry offers a valuable discussion of Kansas's campaign to incarcerate girls with STIs in *Policing Sex in the Sunflower State: The Story of the Kansas State Industrial Farm for Women* (University Press of Kansas, 2021); see page 38 for the quotation on incarcerated girls' immorality cited in the caption to illustration 8.

The Medical Suppression of Incest (ii)

p. 29 ***and another etiology—altogether*** … Physicians' justification for different gender-specific gonorrhea etiologies is briefly discussed in Sacco, 9 and 103–4.

p. 29 ***maintain the idea of virtue as an exclusive possession of white men*** … For a more detailed discussion of the ways the late-19th-century advancement of Black people and dark-skinned immigrants hastened the suppression of incest by white professionals, see Sacco 3, 28, 105–9; *The Washington Post* is quoted on 108.

p. 32 ***many of the themes I have been highlighting emerge again and again*** … Late-20th-century studies promoting or reexamining discredited etiologies of gonorrhea include William B. Shore and Jerry A. Winkelstein, "Nonvenereal Transmission of Gonococcal Infections to Children," *Journal of Pediatrics* 79, no. 4 (1971): 666; Karen S. Israel, Kathleen B. Rissing, and George F. Brooks, "Neonatal and Childhood Gonococcal Infections," *Clinical Obstetrics and Gynecology* 18 (March 1975): 143–5; R. C. Low, C. T. Cho, and B. A. Dudding, "Gonococcal Infections in Young Children," *Clinical Pediatrics* 16 (July 1977): 625–6; James H. Gilbaugh and Peter C. Fuchs, "The Gonococcus and the Toilet Seat," *New England Journal of Medicine* 301 (July 12, 1979): 91; and David P. Ascher, "The Gonococcus and the Toilet Seat Revisited," *Pediatric Infectious Diseases Journal* 8 (March 1989): 191.

p. 33 ***Woody Allen's attorneys relied on them to challenge daughter*** … See the documentary *Allen v. Farrow*, directed by Kirby Dick and Amy Ziering (HBO, 2021). Several commentators, myself included, have argued that Allen's race, wealth, and cultural stature may have shaped how institutions and the public responded to the allegations. Ziering also notes that experts she consulted report that *Allen v. Farrow* was the first high-profile case to employ what is known as the DARVO defense—Deny, Attack, Reverse Victim and Offender. *"In Allen v. Farrow, Woody Allen asserted* *that he himself was the hapless victim, not his child."* See Michele Meek, "The Crime Hidden in Plain Sight: An Interview with Amy Ziering, Director of 'Allen v. Farrow,'" *Ms.*, April 18, 2021 (https://msmagazine.com/2021/04/18/incest-child-abuse-woody-allen-v-farrow-interview-amy-ziering-director/, accessed June 15, 2023).

p. 33 *"false memories" implanted in the daughters* … See Duncan Ways, "Incest Charges Dropped Against Prof, Battery Charges Remain," *The Exponent*, November 27, 2024 (https://www.purdueexponent.org/campus/crime/purdue-professor-incest-charges-dropped/article_a0abf5e6-ac43-11ef-8982-47a5b9cdace7.html, accessed January 13, 2025).

p. 33 *implicating a thermal pool* … See Felicity Goodyear-Smith and Robert Schabetsberger's report implicating crater lake Specchio di Venere "Gonococcus Infection Probably Acquired from Bathing in a Natural Thermal Pool: A Case Report," *Journal of Medical Case Reports* 15, no. 458 (September 17, 2021), (https://jmedicalcasereports.biomedcentral.com/articles/10.1186/s13256-021-03043-6, accessed August 26, 2023).

p. 36 *never is the word "father" mentioned* … The CDC's treatment guidelines and warning signs are available in *"Sexual Assault or Abuse of Children"* (Centers for Disease Control and Prevention, https://www.cdc.

gov/std/treatment-guidelines/sexual-assault-children. html, accessed July 25, 2023).

p. 39 *distribution of penicillin in 1945 did not cure incest* ... For the best available contemporary prevalence figures on gonorrhea vulvovaginitis, see Adaora A. Adimora et al., *Sexually Transmitted Diseases: Companion Handbook*, 2nd ed. (McGraw-Hill, 1994), 354.

p. 39 **because *of her gender*** ... For a forceful discussion of the social formation of heterosexuality as the linchpin of gender oppression, see Catharine A. MacKinnon, "Feminism, Marxism, Method, and the State: An Agenda for Theory," *Signs* 7, no. 3 (1982): 515–544, esp. 530–534.

p. 39 *initiates her life as a sexual subject* ... Incest's value as a patriarchal training ground is perhaps most directly understood by power brokers least concerned with public prestige. When asked what he looks for in his workers, one pimp put it this way: "[B]eauty, yes. Sexual expertise, somewhat. That can be taught easier than you think. What is important above all is obedience. And how do you get obedience? You get obedience if you get women who have had sex with their fathers, their uncles, their brothers—you know, someone they love and fear to lose so that they do not dare to defy"; see Richard Kluft, "On the Apparent Invisibility of Incest," in *Incest-Related Syndromes of Adult Psychopathology* (American Psychiatric Press, 1990), 25.

Incest and the Politics of PTSD

p. 45 ***Augustine wasn't amused by her confinement*** … Because Charcot focused on visually documenting his patients through staged enactments, choreographed demonstrations, sketches, plaster casts, and artfully and professionally composed photos; because the asylum's records are contradictory, incomplete, and often presumptive; and because Charcot was uninterested in women's words, there is little historically accurate information about Augustine's time at the asylum. Useful analyses and reenactments using the bits of information available include Georges Didi-Huberman, *Invention of Hysteria* (MIT Press, 2004), passim; Asti Hustvedt, *Medical Muses: Hysteria in Nineteenth-Century Paris* (W. W. Norton, 2011), 143-211; Elaine Showalter, *The Female Malady: Women, Madness, and English Culture, 1830–1980* (Virago, 2007), 147–154; Alice Winocour, *Augustine* (2012), film; Anna Furse, *Augustine (Big Hysteria)* (Routledge, 1997); and Elizabeth Comen, *All in Her Head: The Truth and Lies Early Medicine Taught Us About Women's Bodies and Why It Matters Today* (Harper Wave, 2024). Augustine's concern about rape and snakes and Charcot's dismissal were, however, recorded and have been variously translated; see Didi-Huberman 161; Showalter 154; and Hustvedt 188–91.

My narrativization is based on the above sources. Few details about Augustine's life prior to and after her confinement exist; see Hustvedt 145–211, but beware the author's mother-blaming.

p. 47 *her "hysterogenital" area* … For Charcot's topography of the female body, including its "hysterogenic zones," see Hustvedt 26.

p. 47 *required naked patients to line up and parade before him* … For more on Charcot's treatment plans, including his choreographed skits involving "hysterical" female patients, see Showalter 148–9.

p. 49 *the "Napoleon of Neuroses"* … Charcot delighted in his nicknames; see Hustvedt 15.

p. 51 *"was as crucial to the study of hysteria as the microscope was to histology"* … See Showalter 149.

p. 53 *"uterine melancholy"* … Melampus's ideas about the etiology of the virgins' discontent can be found in Cecilia Tasca, Mariangela Rapetti, Mauro Giovanni Carta, and Bianca Fadda, "Women and Hysteria in the History of Mental Health," *Clinical Practice and Epidemiology in Mental Health* 8 (2012): 110–19.

p. 54 *women's minds and bodies were second-rate* … The claim that Aristotle's "mutilated" was not meant pejoratively has been made many times (but does not convince me); see Maryanne Cline Horowitz, "Aristotle and Woman," *Journal of the History of Biology* 9, no. 2 (Autumn 1976): 183–213, for a closely argued alternative and a good introduction to feminist rereadings of Aristotle's notions about women.

p. 54 *the uterus becomes unhinged* … I have relied on basic medical histories and feminist rereadings for Hippocrates's ideas about errant uteruses, including Elinor Cleghorn, *Unwell Women: Misdiagnosis and Myth in a Man-Made World* (Dutton, 2021).

p. 54 *"[The uterus] is like an animal within an animal"* … For Aretaeus's ideas about female animism, see Robert Con Davis, "Aristotle, Gynecology, and the Body Sick with Desire" in *Textual Bodies: Changing Boundaries of Literary Representation*, ed. Lori Hope Lefkovitz (State University of New York Press, 1997), 47; see also 35–57 for a useful discussion of Aretaeus's and Hippocrates's ideas about women's psychic distress in the context of Aristotle's.

p. 57 *"Ophelia … is a copy from nature"*… J. C. Bucknill, quoted in Showalter 90.

p. 58 *Tota mulier in utero* … Quoted in Davis 51.

p. 59 *their amygdalae become "dysregulated" and "disorganized"* … For these and related quotations, see Janina Fisher, *The Living Legacy of Trauma Flip Chart* (PESI Publishing, 2022); Janina Fisher, *The Living Legacy of Traumatic Experience* (handout presented at the Brief Therapy Conference, December 9, 2018); B. A. van der Kolk and Rita Fisler, "Dissociation and the Fragmentary Nature of Traumatic Memories: Overview and Exploratory Study," *Journal of Traumatic Stress* 8, no. 4 (1995): 505–25; and van der Kolk, *The Body Keeps the Score: Brain, Mind, and Body in the Healing of Trauma* (Penguin, 2014), passim. M. Harvey quoted in https://cls.unc.edu/wp-content/uploads/sites/3019/2020/02/Flipchart-Diagram-1.pdf, accessed June 14, 2025.

p. 69 *they are biologically more vulnerable to mental distress* … See Paul R. Albert, "Why Is Depression More Prevalent in Women?" *Journal of Psychiatry & Neuroscience* 40, no. 4 (2015): 219–21. Albert's article is especially interesting for the author's echoes of Aretaeus.

p. 69 *result of a preexisting neurological vulnerability* … Quotations regarding the perceived "abnormalities" seen in the brains of sexually traumatized women are from David J. Nutt and Andrea L. Malizia, "Structural and Functional Brain Changes in Posttraumatic Stress Disorder," *Journal of Clinical Psychiatry* 65 (2004): 11–17; Michael D. DeBellis et al., research findings summarized in Judith A. Cohen, Anthony P. Mannarino, and Esther Deblinger, *Treating Trauma and Traumatic Grief in Children and Adolescents* (Guilford, 2006), 14; and Godehard Weniger, Claudia Lange, Ulrich Sachsse, and Eva Irle, "Reduced Amygdala and Hippocampus Size in Trauma-Exposed Women with Borderline Personality Disorder and Without Posttraumatic Stress Disorder," *Journal of Psychiatry & Neuroscience* 34 (2009): 383–88. For a closer look at how some contemporary neurobiological studies devalue women's knowledge and reprivatize girls' and women's experiences of sexual violence, see Emma Jane Tseris, "Trauma Theory Without Feminism? Evaluating Contemporary Understandings of Traumatized Women," *Affilia: Journal of Women and Social Work* 28, no. 2 (2013): 153–64.

p. 70 ***we have to be very alert to who determines the concepts of normality*** ... Concerned about the deterministic assumptions built into medically oriented understandings of women's experience of sexual violence, some feminist social workers and therapists have begun building more positive therapeutic models that incorporate ideas about women's resilience and capacity for joy while acknowledging sexual violence as a form of systemic oppression; see Tseris.

p. 71 ***"raging hormones"*** ... See Gina Rippon, *The Gendered Brain: The New Neuroscience That Shatters the Myth of the Female Brain* (Vintage, 2019),

28–30. For analyses of neuroscientists' continued use of biological essentialism and sexist conventions to confirm conventional gender characteristics, see Cordelia Fine, *Delusions of Gender: How Our Minds, Society, and Neurosexism Create Difference* (W. W. Norton, 2010); Anne Fausto-Sterling, *Myths of Gender: Biological Theories About Women and Men* (Basic Books, 1992) and *Sexing the Body: Gender Politics and the Construction of Sexuality* (Basic Books, 2000); and Caroline Criado Perez, *Invisible Women: Data Bias in a World Designed for Men* (Abrams Press, 2019).

p. 72 ***woman's uterus has "no specific purpose to her life or well-being"*** … See "Rep. Brad Tschida: Uterus a 'Sanctuary' That Serves No Purpose to Women's Own Life," *Daily Montanan*, July 11, 2022, https://dailymontanan.com/2022/07/11/rep-brad-tschida-uterus-a-sanctuary-that-serves-no-purpose-to-womens-own-life/ (accessed June 10, 2025).

p. 72 ***even in cases of incest and rape*** … See *CNN*, February 2, 2025, last modified February 19, 2025, https://www.cnn.com/2025/02/19/politics/ed-martin-justice-department-washington-dc/index.html (accessed June 10, 2025).

p. 72 ***surgically impose ideology on women*** … For a valuable discussion of how Oliver Wendell Holmes and other prestigious eugenicists targeted Buck, see Edwin

Black, *War Against the Weak: Eugenics and America's Campaign to Create a Master Race* (Four Walls Eight Windows, 2003), 108–7 and 120–22.

p. 75 *"child abuse … is the single most preventable cause of mental illness"* … See *The Body Keeps the Score*, 353 and *passim* for other fatuous simplifications.

p. 76 *overrepresentation of women in the psychiatric system* … See Rachel H. Salk, Janet S. Hyde, and Lyn Y. Abramson, "Gender Differences in Depression in Representative National Samples: Meta-Analyses of Diagnoses and Symptoms" *Psychological Bulletin* 143, no. 8 (2017): 783-822.

p. 77 *critics diagnosed Alex in Fatal Attraction … with "erotomania"* … See Tracy Miller, "Glenn Close: My 'Fatal Attraction' Role 'Played Into the Stigma' of Mental Illness" *New York Daily News*, June 4, 2013, https://www.nydailynews.com/life-style/health/glenn-close-fatal-attraction-role-played-stigma-mental-illness-article-1.1362907 (accessed June 10, 2025).

Incest, Sexual Violence, and the Politics of Shame

p. 85 *status degradation, a lowering of rank* … See Gavi S. Ruit, "Rabbinic Commentaries on Genesis

34 and the Construction of Rape Myths," *Journal of Jewish Ethics* 3, no. 2 (2017): 247–66.

p. 85 *in a state of "corruption, a state of harlotry."* … See Ruit 258–59.

p. 86 *"Shame is an originary [original and natural] experience"* … Quoted in Bonnie Mann, "The Difference of Feminist Phenomenology: The Case of Shame," *Puncta* 1 (2018): 41–73; see also 59 for a fuller discussion of Steinbock's account of shame.

p. 86 *"motivate me to reorient my way of living"* … Quoted in Mann 59.

p. 87 *if she was "really a woman."* … See Sally Haslanger, "Changing the Ideology and Culture of Philosophy: Not by Reason (Alone)," *Hypatia* 23, no. 2 (2008): 210–23. (The published text reads "first rate woman philosophy"; "first-rate" and "philosopher" appear here in corrected form.)

p. 88 *81 percent of American women who have experienced some form of sexual assault* … Figures provided by "Statistics," National Sexual Violence Resource Center, https://www.nsvrc.org/statistics, accessed June 8, 2025.

p. 89 ***"defective and misbegotten"*** … See Frank A. James, "Thomas Aquinas on Women," *Carolyn Custis James* (blog), August 6, 2013, https://carolyncustisjames. com/2013/08/06/thomas-aquinas-on-women/ (accessed June 10, 2025).

p. 90 ***"[T]here [is] 'definitely an ick factor,'"*** … Bainbridge made this comment when asked by UCLA law professor Eugene Volokh to comment on Columbia professor David Epstein's incestuous relationship with his daughter. See Matthew J. Franck, "Incest and the Degradation of Our Vocabulary," *Public Discourse*, January 5, 2011 (https://www.thepublicdiscourse. com/2011/01/2316/, accessed June 10, 2025). Of special note is the article's catchy subtitle, "What's Wrong with a Prominent Professor's Incestuous Relationship with His Daughter."

p. 91 ***groundbreaking clinical and cultural examination of incest,* Father-Daughter Incest** … By Judith Lewis Herman (Harvard University Press, 1981).

p. 91 ***"its return to obscurity and silence"*** … Twitchell's argument can be found in Janice Doane and Devon Hodges, *Telling Incest: Narratives of Dangerous Remembering from Stein to Sapphire* (University of Michigan Press, 2001), 135, n. 3.

p. 91 ***"by semantic contagion, leads on to yet worse actions"*** … For a discussion of Hacking's ideas about incest's preternatural agency, see Doane and Hodges, *Telling Incest*, 13.

Where Do We Go from Here?

p. 101 ***disclosed details of her grandfather's incestuous attacks*** … *BBC America* did not air Poppy's story—perhaps preferring to keep it in The Land of Far Away or perhaps simply from indifference—but it is available here (https://www.bbc.com/news/uk-66204893, accessed June 10, 2025) and here (https://www.tiktok.com/@real_life_documentaries/video/7261328264336067867, accessed June 10, 2025).

p. 101 ***pressed into service by the Democratic National Committee*** … See "DNC 2020 Ad | You Matter," YouTube video, posted by Joe Biden, August 17, 2020 (https://www.youtube.com/watch?v=YckKW0hsRiE, accessed June 10, 2025).

p. 103 ***failed to upset the unequal structures of power*** … Herman's groundbreaking study *Father-Daughter Incest* is the first late-20th-century study written from a medical perspective to situate incest in a political context. Other useful studies that explore incest through a sociopolitical lens include Herman's *Trauma and Recovery* (Basic Books, 1992); Jon Olafson, David

Corwin, and Roland Summit; Florence Rush, *The Best Kept Secret: Sexual Abuse of Children* (McGraw-Hill Book Co., 1980); Louise Armstrong, *Kiss Daddy Goodnight: A Speak-Out on Incest* (Hawthorn, 1978) and *Rocking the Cradle of Sexual Politics: What Happened When Women Said Incest* (Addison-Wesley, 1994); Linda Gordon, "'Be Careful About Father': Incest, Girls' Resistance, and the Construction of Femininity," in *Heroes of Their Own Lives: The Politics and History of Family Violence* (University of Illinois Press, 1988); Diana E. H. Russell; and Catharine MacKinnon.

p. 104 ***sexual assault prevention tips for men "Guaranteed To Work!"*** ... Legal Momentum, "Raped or 'Seduced'? How Language Helps Shape Our Response to Sexual Violence," June 1, 2013 (https:// www.legalmomentum.org/LIBRARY/RAPED-OR-%E2%80%9Cseduced%E2%80%9D-how-language-helps-shape-our-response-sexual-violence, accessed June 10, 2025).

p. 107 ***or whether politically decontextualized work is simply another form of oppression*** ... Useful analyses of the limitations of the current medical-diagnostic model as the dominant treatment paradigm include Mary E. Gilfus, "The Price of the Ticket: A Survivor-Centered Appraisal of Trauma Theory," *Violence Against Women* 5 (1999): 1238–57; Debi Brock, "Talkin' Bout a Revelation: Feminist Popular Discourse on Sexual

Abuse," *Canadian Women's Studies / Les Cahiers De La Femme* 12 (1991): 12–15; Bonnie Burstow, "Toward a Radical Understanding of Trauma and Trauma Work," *Violence Against Women* 9 (2003): 1293–1317; and Bonnie Burstow, *Radical Feminist Therapy: Working in the Context of Violence* (Sage Publications, 1992).

LIST OF ILLUSTRATIONS

5. Mother bathing children, 1912. Source: Thomas Herbert Russell and Marshall Everett, *Our Little Men and Women: Modern Methods of Character Building* (Homewood Press, 1912), 177. Image: Library of Congress, via Wikimedia Commons, public domain.

6. Babies Hospital, Medical Center, Broadway & 168th St., New York City, 1930. Photo: Library of Congress, https://www.loc.gov/item/2024691130/.

7. Teenage girls in numbered prison uniforms incarcerated for STIs at the Kansas State Industrial Farm, 1926. Photo: Lansing Historical Society and Museum, Lansing, Kansas.

8. Nathaniel Hawthorne's Hester Prynne, the protagonist of *The Scarlet Letter*, with her daughter Pearl, 1860s. Painting: Hugues Merle. Source: Walters Art Museum, Baltimore.

9. Illustration of poisonous serpent. From *A Comprehensive Dictionary of the Bible*, edited by William Smith, Samuel W. Barnum, et al. (1871).

10. Frederick J. Taussig. Photo: Washington University School of Medicine Oral History Project, Bernard Becker Medical Library.

11. Hospital commode, early 20th century. Photo: Science Photo Library/Alamy Stock Photo.

12. Tidal pool, crater lake Specchio di Venere, Italy. Photo: LaChouettePhoto/iStock.

20. *Pinel Freeing the Insane from their Chains*, 1876. Painting: Tony Robert-Fleury. Source: Wellcome Library Museum.

21. *Ophelia*, 1892. Etching: Madeleine De Lemaire. Source: Leer El Universo.

22. Presidential candidate Hillary Clinton shown on a "lock her up" sign. Source: eBay.

23. Anita Hill testifying before the Senate Judiciary Committee during Clarence Thomas's Supreme Court confirmation hearing, Washington, DC, 1991. Photo: Michael R. Jenkins. Source: https://www.loc.gov/item/201964369/, accessed January 4, 2023.

24. Photo of Pleasance Pendred in *The Suffragette*, ca. 1910s. Source: Sylvia Pankhurst, *The Suffragette*. Source Book Press, 1970; first published by Sturgis & Walton Company, 1911.

25. Official portrait of Christine Lagarde, 2011. Photo: Wikimedia Commons, public domain.

26. Larry Summers, 2005. Photo: © 2024 The Harvard Crimson.

27. Hormone meter. Photo: donskarpo/iStock.

28. Photo of Carrie Buck at the Virginia Colony for Epileptics and Feebleminded, 1924. Photo: A. H. Estabrook. Source: Grenander Special Collections & Archives, University at Albany.

29. Valium ad published in *American Journal of Psychiatry* 121 (1965).

30. Screenshot of Dutch-American psychotherapist Bessel van der Kolk, 2022. Source: How to Detoxify the Body from Trauma (video).

31. Glenn Close as Alex in *Fatal Attraction*. Photo: Paramount Pictures.

32. *The Seduction of Dinah, Daughter of Leah*, ca. 1896–1902. Painting: James Tissot. Source: Gift of the heirs of Jacob Schiff/The Jewish Museum, New York.

33. Sally Haslanger, Ford Professor of Philosophy, MIT, 2013. Photo: Timothy Brown.

34. *St. Aquinas*, 1476. Painting: Carlo Crivelli. Source: The National Gallery, London.

35. *Shame*, 2015. Painting: Andrea Castro. Oil on canvas, 19.7 × 24 × 1.2 in. Spain.

36. Italy's Treccani dictionary. Source: eBay.

37. Screenshot of former Senator Kamala Harris questioning US Attorney General Jeff Sessions in 2017 during a Senate Intelligence Committee hearing. Source: PBS News Hour.

38. Composite of two images: (left) from Andreas Vesalius, *De Humani Corporis Fabrica Libri Septem*, 1543; and (right) from Juan Valverde de Amusco, *Anatomia Humani Corporis*, 1607.

ACKNOWLEDGMENTS

My thanks to Judith Herman for confirming my early sense of things; to Catharine MacKinnon, who offered an incisive word of encouragement when it mattered; to Susan Erlich, who generously shared ideas about the language of rape; and to Christina Vogels, who kindly provided relevant articles on sexual violence. I would also like to thank my old friends Louise Armstrong and Louise de Salvo; the memory of their take-no-prisoners style often acted as a tonic. Thanks also to Cari Shane for her early interest.

I'm also grateful to my editorial team for their research, early commentary, and technical contributions: Grace Roberts, Lisa McHenry Bendel, Beck Siegal, and Mia Innocenti. During the early years of the COVID-19 pandemic, the help of the research staff at the Princeton Public Library in Princeton, New Jersey, was crucial in locating and accessing key historical documents.

I'm especially grateful to Matt Rota and Andrea Castro for graciously allowing me to include their paintings in this book.

Warmest thanks to Alexandra Koken for her early contributions, sustaining interest, and unexpected friendship. Initial copyeditor and rights coordinator, Christopher Lapinski, should be canonized for his patience. His continued interest in this project and his personal and professional help were invaluable.

Special thanks to my publishing consultant, Jeniffer Thompson at Monkey C Media, for her intelligence, creativity, and insights. Her collaboration was essential to the success of this project, her emotional support most welcome.

I'm also grateful to my friends Diana Griebell, Margaret Owens, Vanessa Fell, and Liz Alterman who, early on, laughed. All offered kindness, encouragement, and support.

Deepest thanks to DS for his timely use of the word "hysterical," his galling—and at times outrageous— ignorance, his medical knowledge and insights, his receptivity, and his deep compassion and empathy.

Finally, I want to thank my children—Alana, who listened and listened again, and Alaire, for his sustaining light.

ABOUT THE AUTHOR

Dr. Osborn is a writer and leading cultural critic whose work challenges the stories we are taught to accept as truth. She writes about how power operates in everyday life—through families, institutions, and social norms—to shape what women are allowed to know and say. Known for her clear-eyed, unsentimental style, Osborn takes on subjects often treated as private or unspeakable, showing how silence around violence is maintained and who it ultimately protects.

Her nonfiction books, creative works, and journalistic writing routinely earn praise for their discerning intelligence when tackling difficult subjects. Her essays and criticism have appeared in a wide range of publications, including *The New York Times*, *The Washington Post*, *The Village Voice*, *American Scholar*, and *Chicago Tribune*. Her last nonfiction book, *Elizabeth Bowen: New Critical Perspectives*, was celebrated as a "tour de force;" her last novel, *Surviving the Wreck*, was touted as "a work of genius."

Dr. Osborn currently serves as the director of The Writing Center of Princeton. For many decades, she taught gender, writing, and literature at Rutgers University, Douglass College, The New School for Social Research, and SUNY-New Paltz. After earning her A.B. from Vassar College and her Ph.D. from Rutgers University, she went on to complete additional graduate work at the University of Pennsylvania and Columbia University.

Beyond her academic work, Dr. Osborn serves as a mentor and coach for the Reilly Program at the BOLD Center for Advancing Women's Professional Development at Douglass College and at other colleges and organizations where she addresses the many factors that can disrupt women's professional trajectories, including experiences of sexual violence.

As a public speaker, Dr. Osborn has earned praise for her amiable style and accessible storytelling ability. Her presentations and lectures at universities, literary festivals, and conferences across the US and Europe often explore the cultural and historical foundations of the systemic oppression of women and offer strategies for change.

As an advocate and activist, Dr. Osborn has coordinated initiatives such as the Rutgers' United Nations "16 Days of Activism against Gender-Based Violence" campaign, worked as a consultant for Incest AWARE and as a community educator and speaker for Saprea, an organization combating sexual violence against children.

Feminists, feminist educators and students, social justice advocates, and medical professionals, including psychotherapists, social workers, traumatologists, and emergency room personnel, have taken particular interest in her work for its insightful linkage of past and present injustices and its implications for present-day struggles and reform.

Visit SusanOsborn.net to connect with her to explore book-related opportunities, or to invite her to speak.

LETTER TO THE READER

Dear Reader,

Thank you for spending time with this book. I don't take that lightly. Reading is an act of attention, and your willingness to stay with these ideas—especially those that ask us to look closely at power, silence, and what we've been taught not to name—matters more than I can say.

This book is not meant to be the final word. It is part of an ongoing conversation, one that continues to evolve as we listen more carefully, ask better questions, and resist the comfort of easy explanations. If these pages stirred something in you—curiosity, anger, recognition, resistance, or resolve—I hope you'll stay with that inquiry. Carry it beyond these pages, and let it shape how you listen, question, and respond.

I write regularly on my blog, where I continue to explore these themes and respond to the world as it unfolds. You're warmly invited to join me there, and to follow along on social media as well. You can find everything at susanosborn.net.

Thank you again for reading, for thinking, and for being willing to engage. Conversations like this only happen because readers like you choose to show up.

With appreciation,
Susan Osborn